The BIG RUN

Life Aboard a Salmon Seiner

RAY FADICH

Caxton Press

First Edition
ISBN # 978-087004-6339
Library of Congress Control Number: 2020936751

CIP Information available at Loc.gov

Cover and book design by Jocelyn Robertson

Printed in the United States of America
CAXTON PRESS
Caldwell, Idaho
206889

In memory to my father

The cast, clockwise from top center:

GENE WAKELL – the cocky, dissipated engineer
SAM (SEAGULL-EYE) FADICH – the keen-eyed 1st mate
BOB SANDERS – the portly, good-natured cook
RAY (RAYMONDO) FADICH – the greenhorn skiffman
JOHN PADOVAN – deckhand
NELS NELSON – the quiet, reserved deckhand
TOM MARINCOVICH – the serious, conforming, operator of the skiff
PAUL ZANKICH – the veteran, old salt of the crew
NICK (FOREIGNER) BARHANOVICH (center) – the boisterous skipper

AUTHOR'S NOTE

WHEN I SAT DOWN TO WRITE THIS BOOK,
I wondered if I could recall events that happened over forty years ago. I was amazed at the mind's power to store information. As I wrote, details of the events came back in vivid fashion – as if they happened only recently. In a way, it was like living 1958 – an incredible year – over again.

As in all works, credit must be shared with those who lent a helping hand. A special thanks to: Ethel Dassow (proof-reading and editing); Nikki Keating (computer and layout); Burt Fadich (some of the photographs).

INTRODUCTION

DURING THE HEYDAY OF COMMERCIAL
fishing, when a fisherman threw his seabag
aboard a fishing vessel he anticipated a banner
year. What else would keep him coming back to
endure the hard work, long hours, grimy living
conditions and oftentimes dangerous seas? The
dream of the bonanza catch was the inducement
that kept him coming back year after year, the
one big catch, or two, that would make his season.
When fishing is good, a fisherman tends to forget
about the harsh conditions; but when fishing is
poor, it can weigh heavy on his mind. At the end
of a poor season, a fisherman may shoulder his
seabag with the intention of never again setting
foot aboard a fishing vessel. However, by the next
spring, as the fishing season approaches, he has
forgotten the hardships and the poor season, and
once again is dreaming of the bonanza.

The habitual dreamer, a fisherman lives
with an obsession, and clings to optimism, en-
visioning a day of grandeur. In fishing, there is
a passion that can capture a man's soul; once
instilled, it's difficult to remove. Of course, not
every person has the makeup to be a fisherman,
but the ones that do form a love for it; they love
the adventure, the unknown, the gamble of being
free-spirited individuals. Sometimes they receive
rich rewards for their freedom, other times they
pay for it.

Not every season is a good one, not every
boat catches fish. However, a fisherman knows
a season can be made in a few days of good
fishing, and on occasion good money can be
made in a single day. He also knows of incidents
where expenses have exceeded revenue from
fish caught, leaving the crew high and dry with

nothing to show for their months of hard labor.
Knowing these two extremes, a fisherman figures
that at worst, he'll fall somewhere in between; but
there's always that lingering dream swimming in
his mind—the bonanza. He'd be kicking himself
for the rest of his life if he missed that.

The focus of Puget Sound commercial
fishermen is the sockeye salmon. Of the five
species of salmon, the sockeye is the most highly
prized by fishermen and the canning industry.
Why? Because this six-pound treasure has the
reddest flesh of all the salmon. The rich, red color,
together with outstanding flavor, is preferred by
the consumer and brings the highest price for
canned salmon.

The king salmon, known in some areas
as chinook or tyee, is widely acclaimed as the
monarch of the Pacific salmon. It is by far
the biggest of them. Fifty-pounders are not
uncommon, and an occasional specimen has
weighed a hundred pounds or more. Its flesh is
usually reddish, sometimes white (no one knows
what causes the difference), and its flavor is highly
palatable.

If the king is the monarch, then the
sockeye is the crown prince. It is small compared
to the king—an average of six pounds, twenty-six
inches long, but much more uniform than the king
in size. Its streamlined body, with its blue-green
back and silver belly, is well adapted for speed
and maneuverability. Strange though it may
seem, the sockeye has no teeth. It feeds mainly on
plankton, which is why it eludes the commercial
troller and the sports fisherman. Perhaps that is
also why it tends to be free of sea lice and other

parasites that attack most fish species. If there is such a thing as an elegant fish, it's the sockeye.

Sockeye differ from other salmon species because they require a lake-like environment for part of their life. They spawn in the gravel of streams, then as fry migrate upstream or downstream to a lake-like habitat. As fingerlings they occupy this habitat for one to two years before migrating to the ocean as smolts. After their stay in the ocean, where they feed on rich plankton, the adult sockeye return to the river of their birth. Returning sockeye from the Pacific enter Puget Sound, then head for their spawning grounds in the Fraser River system in British Columbia where they spawn and die.

The life cycle of sockeye is four years, meaning a sockeye born this year will return in four years to spawn and die. Although sockeye run every year in Puget Sound, records show that, in the past, every fourth year a big run developed. The reason for this no one knows for sure. Was it a fluke of nature, or ideal conditions in the lake during the fry and fingerling stage? Was ocean nourishment more favorable, or were there better conditions in the river during migration?

Whatever the reason, at the turn of the century, the odd-cycle years of 1897, 1901, 1905, 1909, and 1913 had bonanza sockeye runs—the best sixteen years of the Fraser River system. In 1913, forty million sockeye returned to the Fraser and thirty million were caught by fishermen. It was by then the world's largest producing river of sockeye salmon.

However, something happened in 1913 that would change the destiny of the sockeye. Hell's Gate, a place appropriately named, lay in the path of those millions of returning sockeye. One hundred twenty miles from the mouth of the Fraser, Hell's Gate was a narrow, rocky canyon barely one hundred feet wide. The water from the Fraser's ninety thousand square mile watershed funneled through this narrow gap with roaring velocity. In 1913 the canyon reverberated with other sounds: the noise of heavy equipment, the thunder of dynamite, the rumbling of rock avalanches. The construction of a railroad bed was being built with no thought of the consequences. Tons of rock were blasted away with no regard to the salmon.

The narrow canyon was made narrower by the debris, making conditions extremely difficult for the salmon. The swifter water made passage nearly impossible; millions of exhausted sockeye were swept downstream to die, unable to negotiate the agitated waters of Hell's Gate.

The few sockeye that made it were to face yet another traumatic challenge. A logging operation was allowed to build a splash dam across the upper Adams River, a tributary of the Fraser, which proved to be devastating to the sockeye. The combination of Hell's Gate blockage and the Adams River dam practically annihilated the Adams River sockeye run. It was to be more than thirty years before these obstructions on the rivers were improved to restore easier passage for the sockeye. It's not surprising the next few cycles of the run were alarmingly low.

By the time the 1940s rolled around, the big-run cycles had switched to even years. Another quirk of nature? Or was it the fact that since the odd-year cycle had been nearly annihilated, another cycle had found favorable conditions to prosper? In any event, the years 1942, 1946, 1950 and 1954 produced big runs, providing good expectations for the next cycle in 1958.

It is important for the reader to understand that in 1958, and in the years before, commercial fishermen were considered farmers of the sea. Instead of harvesting wheat from the rolling hills of eastern Washington, their crop was salmon from the cool waters of Puget Sound. Commercial fishermen normally worked five days a week with weekends off, like shore-workers did.

Purse-seining and gillnetting, the two traditional methods of harvesting salmon, have been used on Puget Sound since the late 1800s. Over the years, they have proved to be efficient means to catch salmon. Because of the large runs in the past, it was necessary to can the majority of the salmon and ship the canned salmon world-wide. That was the only way to distribute a harvest of the magnitude being caught.

Today, we face a different challenge; canning is not the only option. With the smaller runs and a much larger human population in the Pacific Northwest, it is possible to distribute much of the salmon in the fresh and frozen markets locally. What can't be sold locally can be air-freighted to markets elsewhere.

In 1958, about four hundred seine boats and one thousand gillnet boats plied the waters of Puget Sound in the quest for salmon. There was never a serious conflict between the sport fishermen and commercial fishermen at the time. There was enough fish for both. The sportsmen understood the commercial fishermen were making a living, while the commercial fishermen figured the sportsmen had the right to catch their own salmon.

Sixteen years later, however, in 1974, a change came about that would drastically change the fisheries of Puget Sound. In what became known as the "Boldt Decision," a judge gave Indian fishermen the right to fifty percent of the harvestable salmon. The judge interpreted the wording "in common" in an 1855 treaty between the whites and Indians to mean that each group would be entitled to half the catch. The Indian fishermen were a small percentage of the fleet, so the ruling created a huge imbalance in the catch—ten percent of the fleet would catch fifty percent of the salmon. This left the white fishermen at a huge disadvantage; many could no longer make a living.

By 1974 the salmon runs had already begun their decline. The only way to save the runs was to enforce strict regulations on all means of fishing on Puget Sound. Today, commercial fishermen, sport fishermen and Indian fishermen must all make sacrifices to ensure salmon for the future.

The salmon fishery in Puget Sound is much different now than in 1958, when the story you are about to read took place. In the 1950s, the industry was still comparatively healthy. Fishermen were still making a living at fishing, which is not the case today. The commercial salmon industry has suffered dramatic changes over the past twenty years. Declining runs, loss of habitat, lower prices brought about by developing fish farms, and too many people wanting a piece of the shrinking salmon pie are factors leading to the problems of today. It's a simple and proven fact: industrial progress, along with population sprawl, are not compatible with salmon. It's no wonder the wild salmon stocks are becoming alarmingly low.

Today, many commercial fishing boat owners would sell their boats if buyers were available, as it is difficult or near impossible to take an expensive boat with high operating costs to the fishing grounds for a few hours of fishing and a meager return. In fact, fishermen on the docks now refer to purse seining as "sport seining"—a way of expressing their frustration.

In the pastt—and this is what this book is about—it was a much different story. Instead of the doom and gloom of today, there was hope and anticipation.

Now that you have a synopsis of the fishermen and fishing, let's step back in time to the year 1958. You are welcome aboard the sixty-foot purse seine boat, *Emancipator*. Join the crew of eight, and travel with them through an epic fishing season. While aboard, learn the ways of the fishermen, and get an inside look at the commercial fishing industry of Puget Sound.

According to the trend of a "big run" every four years, the next big run was due in 1958. Would records hold true and the trend continue in the year 1958? The story you are about to read will reveal the facts.

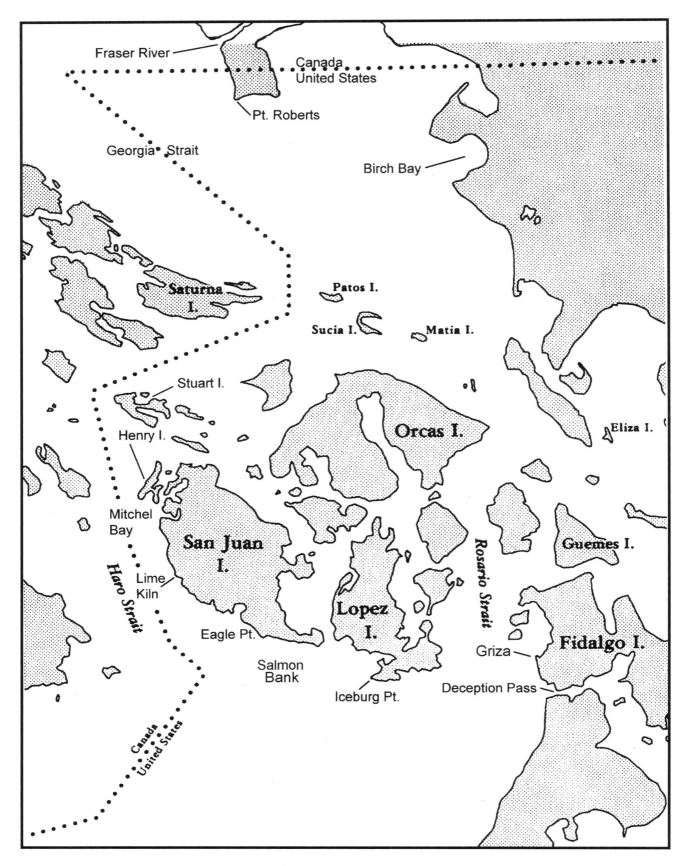

Fishing areas in Puget Sound for sockeye salmon.

TABLE OF CONTENTS

Freshly painted seiners are prepared for season to open.

THE HIRING

WITH THE DREARY, WET DAYS COME THE
winter blues. Darkness shrouds the Northwest by
four thirty p.m., and the daylight does not replace
it until eight a.m. In addition, during those short
rations of daylight, overcast skies block the refreshing rays of the sun, or dark, ominous clouds
pelt the ground with relentless rain. The pro-
longed darkness has a way of draining the soul.

My job, in a cold building (kept that way
to preserve the freshness of seafood) only adds to
the drudgery. My task is to clean the crabs, shuck
clams, slice or fillet fish, and perform any other
slimy, smelly, chilly chore required in an old-
fashioned fish market. This market, owned by my
dad, is one of the last to survive a modernistic
society. One by one, independent shops have
locked their doors in favor of pre-packaging in
the supermarkets.

In Dad's market, you make money the
old-fashioned way. You earn it. With limited
refrigeration space, most of the stock is kept on
crushed ice in a front-window display. I have to
dig continually into the ice to satisfy a customer's
wish. The combination of the cold building and
the ice chills me to the bone. When I am digging
into the ice, my hands feel as if they are suffering
the first stages of frostbite.

I am still a rank amateur in the fish
handling business compared to the master.
Dad is a wizard with the knife. When he
finishes filleting a fish, there's not enough flesh
left on the backbone to satisfy a fly. In addition,
Dad seems to have hands of steel. He can
work for hours with his hands in the ice, with
no apparent discomfort. I have to run to the
warmth of the back room after working in the

ice for just a few minutes.

The back room is my savior. It contains an
old wood stove with a fire always burning and
radiating pleasurable heat. A door separates the
back room from the retail part of the store. In
the dead of winter it can be forty degrees in the
retail part, where no heat is allowed, while the
back room can be a steamy eighty-five.

Another inducement to linger in the back
room is Dad's collection of more than a hundred
girlie calendars hanging on its walls. His collection,
saved over a period of several years, is renowned,
and he has numerous friends who venture into
the back room. There is always hot coffee on the
stove, and a tray of glazed doughnuts, a watering
hole with intriguing amenities.

During slow retail times, and when most of
the routine work is done (which is not often), the
back room is the place to be. The front door is
connected to a bell, so we can always hear when
someone enters. While I am riding out the winter,
my mind often dwells upon thoughts of acquiring
an outside job for the coming summer. Being
cooped up for long periods of time is against my
nature.

One day while I am weighing a few kippers
for a customer, Foreigner Nick (owner and skipper
of the seine boat *Emancipator*) comes barging
through the door.

"Get your damn hand off that scale, you
little bastard!" he bellows on his way to the back
room. My customer looks stunned, but then
he realizes that the lion's roar is only a friendly
greeting. He turns to me and smiles.

Nick is noted for his loud mouth and cutting

tongue, and is called "Foreigner" because of his old-country accent. He often comes by to lend atmosphere to the back room and drink coffee. When he is in the building there's no mistake about it. His voice reverberates within the brick walls like a belching rhino's.

After finishing with the customer, I go to the back room to warm my hands on the stove.

"I hear you're looking for an outside job," Foreigner barks, as he blows a cloud of cigar smoke in my direction.

"Yeah, know of any?"

"Do you have any experience?" he asks.

"Five summers of gillnetting on the Columbia River, with three of the best: Cap Bozanich, Nick Bozanich, and Nick Marincovich."

Foreigner gets up from his chair, lifts the circular lid on the stove, and spits some cigar juice into the fire. "That's all fine and good, but seining is a lot different from gillnetting. Have you ever seined?"

"No."

Sitting back down on the chair, Foreigner looks me up and down as he chews on the stub of his cigar. He rocks the chair back on its hind legs, still eyeing me. "I understand you ran a gillnet boat on Puget Sound last summer," he says. "Do any good?"

"I tried."

Foreigner is uncharacteristically silent for a few moments, then says, "I'm looking for a skiff-man. I suppose if you can run a gillnet you can run a skiff."

The bell on the front door rings, so I go out to wait on a customer. While I'm with the customer, Foreigner comes out of the back room to leave. "We'll hang the seine the first part of June," he says. "See you then."

"Okay, Captain!"

During the following weeks, as I work in the fish market, my thoughts wander often to the upcoming fishing season. Having been around fishermen most of my twenty-seven years on this planet, I have some knowledge of purse seining. In five summers of gillnetting on the Columbia, and talking to other fishermen on the docks, I have learned the basics of the seining operation. In contrast to gillnetting, which is done at night, purse seining is done during the daylight hours. Seiners have cooks aboard who serve fantastic meals. Gillnetters get by with makeshift grub. A seine boat has a crew of eight to scuttlebutt with, whereas a gillnetter is alone to fend for himself.

What intrigues me is knowing that most seining is done around the San Juan Islands of northern Puget Sound, a beautiful place to be during the summer. Thoughts of being out there in the fresh air have this caged lion eager to go through a door that has been left ajar.

A person can hear a lot about an operation, but he doesn't really know it until he has actually done it. Knowing this, I'm somewhat anxious about this new challenge. Eager though I am to meet it, I've heard wild tales about purse seine skippers whose behaviors range from benevolent to the bizarre, running even to lunacy. Where my skipper belongs on this scale, I don't know yet.

THE HANGING

JUNE ARRIVES AND FOREIGNER NOTIFIES members of his crew to assemble at his net shed, located on the 14th Street dock in Everett, to hang the seine. It is a week before the sockeye salmon season opens. Before the fishing season starts, the seine must be carefully prepared. The success of a fishing season may depend on this care in preparation. All the strips of the seine are laced together by hand with a special heavy twine. A cork line is sewn around the top edge of the seine with enough corks on the line to keep it afloat, even with a load of fish. Along the bottom of the seine is a lead line, shorter than the cork line, to make the seine hang vertical, giving the seine a concave shape. Along the weighted lead line are bridles, which hang down below about thirty inches. Each bridle holds a brass ring, through which the purse line runs and is drawn through.

The operation to "purse up," or close the seine, is done by hauling the purse line aboard the boat with powerful winches. After the seine is gradually closed it is pulled aboard the boat, with the fish being caught and retained in the "money bag," or bundt. A strong boom on the boat is used to brail the fish from the seine into the hull storage. The brailer is a large dip net with an attached ten-foot handle, by which the brailer is steered through the mass of fish, scooping them up at about a half-ton at a time.

During hanging is a time for the crew members to get acquainted. Sometimes the crew of a particular boat will change almost to the man, but normally most crewmen are holdovers from the previous season. A boat with a good reputation for catching fish usually has little turnover. The crewman's wages are a percentage of the total take, so fishermen are likely to stay with a highline skipper.

The Everett fleet of purse seiners numbers about twenty. Each employs a crew of eight: skipper, engineer, cook, first mate, two deckhands, and two skiffmen. The crews are chosen from a pool of experienced fishermen numbering fewer than two hundred. If a skipper needs a new crewman, he looks to the pool. He wants experienced hands; they make the hard task of working a seine easier.

Each year a few newcomers, or greenhorns, enter the pool, but it is difficult to crack the shell that surrounds this elite group. On occasion even a person with no experience will land a job. This usually occurs only if there is a sudden sickness or a no-show, and there is no one readily available from the pool. Once a novice gets a season's experience, it will be easier for him to get another job. Then, after he has gained a few years of experience and a reputation for a good work ethic, a skipper will come to seek him rather than the other way around. Since the pool is relatively small, a man's reputation is known quickly within the fleet.

All of Foreigner's crewmen are holdovers except me. This means that on this first day of hanging, I will face six strangers, and a skipper that I scarcely know. I am wild with anticipation, and feel like a Christian about to be thrown to the lions. My little VW bug has difficulty getting started, so I arrive a few minutes after Foreigner's designated starting time. I park the bug behind the net sheds, then hasten to shed Number 2. I

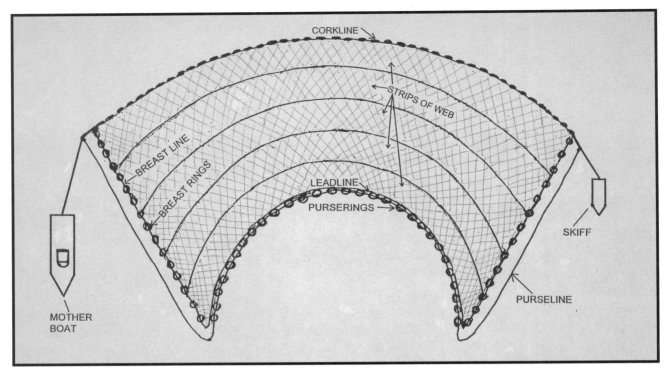

The workings of a purse seine — It stretches the length of six football fields: it's depth from corkline to leadline is 80 feet. The mother boat and skiff tow seine until circle is completed, then purseline is drawn in closing bottom and entrapping salmon.

enter through the big double doors and see the crew working busily on the seine.

Foreigner, sewing a section of seine, spots me and announces loudly to the crew, "Look boys, the king has arrived, everyone bow to his majesty." No bows, just amused countenance from the crew.

I await my orders. Foreigner looks at me scornfully then jerks the seine I'm standing on sending me sprawling to the floor. "Get off your butt and fill some needles," he orders. Regaining my feet, I look for needles but can't see any.

"I'll be darn, I hired a blind man," Foreigner scoffs, "Get the rope boys, we'll hang him from the rafters."

At this point I'm about to tell Foreigner to take this job and shove it, but I have a family to feed so I must endure.

The crew, accustomed to Foreigner's behavior, merely smiles at one another. I don't know whether they're smiling in appreciation of Foreigner's humor or in sympathy for me.

Foreigner barges over to me and grabs a needle from the shelf on the wall.

"*This,*" he says, "is a needle." He hands it to me and picks up a ball of twine. "*This,*" he says, "is twine. You hold the needle in your left hand, and with your right hand you wrap the twine around the needle. Do you think you can do that, *boozdoe?*" (dumbbell).

"I'll try," I answer. By now my pride is kicking in. "I've only filled a couple thousand on the Columbia River."

"Oh," Foreigner shouts, "he's not a *boozdoe*, he's a wise ass!" He storms away shaking his head in disgust.

Foreigner moves around the net shed, measuring lengths of web and giving instructions. The seine, three hundred fathoms (eighteen hundred feet) long, is piled at the far end of the shed. The shed is ten fathoms long, so it will take thirty stretches, or pulls, to go through the entire seine. After each pull, the web of the seine is attached to the lead line and to the cork line. Between these two lines are five strips of web which must be laced together. When it's all put

Spring – 1958. Seine boats wait quietly for another season. A portion of Everett's purse seine fleet.

together, this seine could wrap around two city blocks, making a fence sixty feet high.

At the close of the salmon season, the seine is stripped down. The cork line and lead line are cut from the seine, and five to seven strips of web are disassembled and separated. Each spring, during the "hanging" of the seine, the entire operation is reversed. There are also many brass rings, about six inches in diameter, attached to the lead line. The purse line runs through these rings. When the seine is in a "set"—or "haul"—on the fishing grounds, the purse line gathers the bottom edge of the seine so the salmon can't escape by swimming or diving under the seine. The seine works much like a woman's drawstring purse, which is where it got its name.

Sitting there filling needles, I watch the crew. One man is hanging the cork line, another is hanging the lead line, and four others are lacing strips of web together. Foreigner shuttles over to me, removes his hat, and whacks me on the back of the head with it. I wonder if he's practicing for the coming season.

"Faster, you little bastard," he says.

It takes about one hour to hang the ten fathoms of each pull. Than all eight of us work together to pull those ten fathoms the length of the shed, across the blacktop floor. On the boat, we'll have a hydraulic block to pull the seine, but in the shed it is strictly manpower.

While we strain our guts pulling the seine across the floor, Foreigner shouts, "Pull hard and it'll come easy," or, "Pull 'til you're blue in the face, then pull harder!" Oh, how Foreigner loves to yell. He is at the height of his glory when his strident voice carries out the big double doors at the end of the shed. Those working on the dock know he's just a big bag of wind, but the occasional passer-by must think there's a raving lunatic in the building. The carry-over crew is accustomed to his showmanship, and they merely look at one another and smile indulgently at his insults. I've yet to learn how to take them, and of course I, as the greenhorn, am being tested.

Although Foreigner has been in the United States for twenty years, he hasn't shaken his Croatian influence. He's a loquacious man. His corpulent belly and inevitable cigar are familiar on the Everett waterfront. If one voice is heard above the others on the dock, you may be sure it's his. Yet, it's been said that in a one-to-one situation, he speaks softly, with the gentleness of a small-town minister. It seems that a crowd automatically triggers his bellicose behavior.

Most of the skippers are reserved, and demand respect from their crews. To them fishing is serious business. Foreigner, the odd one, likes to temper hard work with a little raillery.

Now, in the late nineteen-fifties, the skipper-crew relationship is changing. It wasn't so many years ago, the old-timers say, that the skipper was Mr. Almighty. Back then, crewmembers were expected to cut wood for the skipper's fireplace in the winter, and in the spring, paint his house. They were also expected to spend a month or more cleaning and painting the boat—all this for the chance at the coming season.

"Easy for you," the old-timers often say to the newcomers. They speak nostalgically of "the old days" of wooden ships and iron men—the way things used to be. They speak of the days before the power block, how they pulled the heavy, sopping-wet, cotton seine over the stern until their arms and back drained and pained. "Easy for you," they say of the light nylon web and lines, the power blocks, the plastic corks, "but back then…."

No question about it, if the fleet of today had to revert to those old methods, not one boat could get a crew. Some of the survivors of the old days are now seen on the docks, dragging their feet along, hunched over in the picking position. Retired now, physically unfit for work, still they respond to the lure of the waterfront.

The back-saver of the fishing industry is the Marco Power Block, designed by another Croatian immigrant; it alleviated the need to hand-haul the water-soaked seine over the stern. Mario Puretic worked as a commercial fisherman in Southern California, fishing sardines, anchovy and mackerel. He saw the effects of the heavy hauling in the twisted spines of fisherman grown old before their time. While other fishermen merely complained, Puretic did something about it. He designed a hydraulic spool for the seine to run through, and located it high on the boom. It could pull the seine from the water and through the block to the waiting crew at the stern. The hardest work was over.

Puretic's invention revolutionized the industry. In only a few years, almost all the Puget Sound fleet had made the conversion. Even the conservative skippers and the hard-nosed skeptics could not turn their backs for long.

THE CREW

WE WORK ON THE SEINE UNTIL NOON, then gather for lunch in the galley of the *Emancipator*, tied alongside the dock. Bob, the cook, has soup and cold-cut sandwiches waiting for us. He has fired up the galley stove, an old-fashioned flat-top Olympic, which runs on diesel fuel. The galley is uncomfortably hot. We sit around the table.

"You guys better like this homemade soup," Bob says as he ladles it out. "I had to slave over a hot stove all morning to make it."

"Looks like Campbell's to me," Gene, the engineer, says sarcastically.

Bob, displaying a pretended look of bewilderment and hurt, says, "You mean to tell me that my homemade soup, with its secret herbs and spices, can be confused with Campbell's?"

Tom, the skiffman, who's six foot three, towers over the rest of us. From his altitude he can peer over heads and into the galley sink. In it he spies a large can. "What's so secret about Heinz?" he asks.

"Well, so much for my secret herbs and spices," Bob laments. Then he starts laughing so heartily that his robust belly shakes. "Sorry, boys, but our budget doesn't allow T-bones until we start making some money."

"They're damned lucky to get this," Foreigner declares, reaching for a bologna sandwich. "They haven't earned their keep yet." He turns to me, the greenhorn, and between husky bites of his sandwich explains, "Once we're out on the fishing grounds we'll eat like kings. Steaks, roasts, *pasta fasul*, fish, nothing but the best. But you'll earn every mouthful."

Today's is a leisurely lunch. There won't be time for such luxury, once the season is in progress.

"Enjoy it, boys," Foreigner says. "When we're fishing we have to eat like seagulls. No chewing. Just bite and swallow."

Gene, the arrogant one, remarks sarcastically, "With this kind of grub, that's the best way."

The crew is a diversified group, ranging in age from nineteen to sixty-five. Paul, the oldest, is considered the "old salt," not only by our crew, but also by the entire fleet. He is respected by the veterans and held in awe by the younger fishermen. His stories of the "good ol' days" are legendary, and for a man his age, his physical feats are astonishing. One of his favorites is chinning himself twenty times in rapid succession on the tight hawser that connects the seine to the boat when it's under tow. When he's finished he'll strut about the deck, like a proud rooster in a flock of hens. "I'd do it a hundred times," he'll boast, "but I don't want to make you young punks feel like sissies." During a storm, when he's decked out in oilskins and sou'wester, Paul is said to be the personification of the commercial fisherman.

Next oldest is Sam, at fifty-three. He is also noted for his physical feats. His favorite is walking on his hands the entire length of the net shed. In his younger days he could negotiate stairs and hills, but he now limits his exhibitions to flat surfaces. Sam is noted for his keen eyesight. It's claimed that he can spot a jumping salmon three-quarters of a mile away, and distinguish it as a sockeye or a humpy. This faculty has earned him the name of Seagull Eye. He's about five foot six. He has John L. Lewis eyebrows and the energy of a barrel of wildcats.

Sam has fished for many years. One incident from his past haunts him. While he was gillnetting on the Columbia River, he had a quarrel with his skipper and got left on the beach to "walk the rails." Curiously enough, that skipper was his father-in-law to be. A wise skipper will overlook this blemish on Sam's reputation in consideration of his keen eye for *riba* (fish) and his dependable work ethic. Sam has been around the fishing industry longer than most skippers have. This alone warrants a listening ear.

Nelson, known as "the Quiet Norwegian," or simply Nels, is a master deckhand. It will be his job to release the pelican hook when the skipper yells "Mola!" from the flying bridge. At this command, which means, "Let go!", Nels will pull on a short line attached to the pelican hook, releasing it so it will release the skiff, which in turn starts pulling the seine off the stern of the mother boat. This series of acts initiates a "set," or "haul." Nels, who's about forty-five, is most likely the best seaman on board. He is a quiet man whose response to happenings on board is usually a meek, innocent smile. His shyness may result from the fact that six men of the crew have surnames that end in "ich," a clue to their Croatian ancestry. Nels, as the lone Norwegian, may feel like a lamb among wolves.

Bob, the cook, is a well-rounded man, about two hundred and fifty pounds, in his middle forties. Fishermen who have crewed with Bob tell other fishermen to be on the alert, for Bob's real love in life is pulling off some good-natured trick. When you hear his hearty, barrel-chested laugh and see his whole rotund body shaking, you can be sure he has pulled off some prank. He gets serious long enough to put together a meal that no other cook in the fleet can top, and judging from his size, he's his own best customer.

Gene, the engineer, who's thirty, seems to subsist on caffeine and nicotine. They say that a sight of Gene without a coffee cup in his hand or a cigarette in his mouth, or both, is as rare a sight as George Burns without a cigar. He seems aloof, haughty, even arrogant, but the crew will just have to live with that. Gene's job on board will be to maintain and operate the Caterpillar diesel engine, located in the hull beneath the galley.

Of course the alpha star of the crew is Foreigner. He is unique. His reputation for "embellishing" the English language is renowned throughout the fleet. His sharp tongue can reduce a man from six foot three to five foot nine with a single phrase. On the rare occasion when Foreigner has to listen to someone else, he picks nervously at the hair on his left arm, which leaves the arm noticeably bare. He loves his vino, and when he's indulging, his nose and cheeks become almost as red as the vino. Though he is not yet forty, his belly has already reached stupendous size. The consensus of the crew is that if either Foreigner or the cook should fall into the hold, it will take the double block to rescue him. Eccentric though he is, Foreigner manages to catch his share of fish.

The skiff requires a crew of two, usually the two crewmen with the least experience. The job is the first step on the way up the seniority ladder. The skiffman is expected to take verbal abuse from the higher-ups in the pecking order. It's like an initiation to test his resilience. If he can endure one season of abuse he becomes a man—a fisherman. Then, after another season or two, it's the skiffman's turn to move up the pecking order, join the crew on the mother boat. Bitter and resentful from the abuse he has taken, he can now release his hostilities on the new skiffmen. It's a vicious cycle, but it is an established institution in the industry.

The two skiffmen are expected to get into the skiff at four in the morning, and for the next sixteen hours they're separated from the mother boat. The skiff is either towing one end of the seine, or towing the mother boat clear from the pursed-up seine. When the skiff is towing the mother boat, one skiffman jumps aboard to help in picking up the seine.

Though it's called a skiff, the craft used here is far from what the layman pictures—a

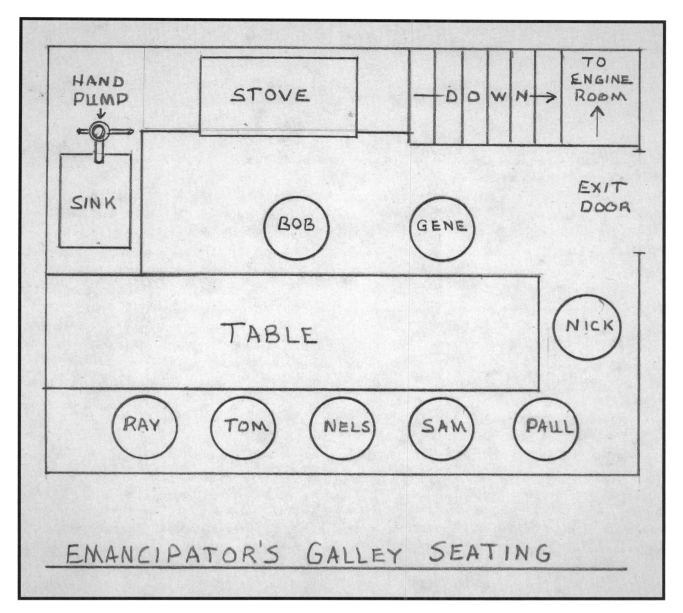

HAND PUMP

STOVE

←D|O|W|N→ TO ENGINE ROOM ↑

SINK

EXIT DOOR

BOB

GENE

NICK

TABLE

RAY TOM NELS SAM PAUL

EMANCIPATOR'S GALLEY SEATING

small rowboat. It is a rugged boat, designed for use with a powerful engine. It may have as much pulling power as the mother boat.

Tom and I are the skiffmen. Tom, the youngest of the crew at nineteen, is a college student who hopes to earn enough during the fishing season to finance another year in school. He is a tall, healthy-looking lad with curly blond hair. He will be in the driver's seat of the skiff, and his duties are maintaining and operating it. Having fished the previous season with Foreigner, Tom has already endured a season of the abuse and put-downs that are the lowly skiffman's lot.

Me—I'm at the bottom of the pecking order. Having fished on gillnet boats on the Columbia, I am not a complete greenhorn in the ways of fish and fishermen. Nevertheless, purse seining is a different ballgame. I have a lot to learn, and it's my turn to be used and abused.

The crew, now assembled in the galley, is seated in the order we will adhere to throughout the season, another established practice in the industry. However, there's a practical reason for the arrangement. The cook sits near the stove for obvious reasons. The engineer sits next to the cook for easy access to the engine room, in case he has to attend to the engine. The skipper sits at the head of the table, near the door, so he can

9

monitor activities outside. The rest of us sit along the inside wall according to choice or seniority. I, having neither, am landlocked in the least desirable seat. My only chance to escape is when the five men who block my exit have finished eating and leave.

After lunch the crew climbs dockside, back to hanging the seine. The dock is now crowded with people. Five Everett boats are readying to leave for False Pass, in the Aleutians. Wives, children, other relatives and friends have gathered to bid them farewell. The five boats are *Dreamland, Freeland, Iceland, Wonderland,* and *St. Christopher.* Their five skippers—Paul, Tony, and Matt Martinis, and Matt and Andy Marincovich— are two sets of brothers who have been going north for many years. They make the eighteen hundred-mile trip to fish the stormy waters of the Bering Sea—always a tough three months for the fishermen, but the monetary gains usually compensate for the hardships.

Back in the net shed, the eight of us begin where we left off with the seine. Each hour is a repetition of the hour before—hang ten fathoms, pull and pile.

On the third day, with the seine coming along on schedule, the skipper has me do some work on the boat. The aging *Emancipator* was built in 1917. Foreigner bought her two years ago from the cannery he's been fishing for the last several years. He has put money and work into her restoration, a little each year, but many things still need to be done. I notice, while working in the hold, that the stuffing box is leaking profusely. Thinking this is a problem that needs attention, I yell to the skipper, "This stuffing box is leaking like hell!" Foreigner looks down into the hatch and says, "Only normal, my boy. A boat needs a little water to keep her tight, just like a man needs a few glasses of wine every day."

Looking at the hull from the inside, I notice the paint is blistered and falling away in places, and I see daylight through some of the higher seams. "What about these seams?" I ask. "I can see daylight through some of them."

"A boat needs air," Foreigner explains, "so she can smell fresh, like a perfumed lady."

"I don't think this hold will smell like perfume when it's full of fish!"

"My boy," Foreigner declares, "if that hold ever gets full of fish, it'll be the sweetest thing you'll ever smell!"

"How much will she hold?"

"Don't know," Foreigner admits. "She's never been full."

"You mean she's never been plugged?"

"Not that I know of. However, she's forty years old, so maybe she has been sometime."

"It's chiseled here on the hatch combing," I say, "that her maximum capacity is forty tons."

"The way fishing is nowadays," Foreigner says ruefully, "we'll never find out for sure."

At the rear of the hold is the lazaret, a dark, dingy chamber where various pieces of gear and spare parts are stored. The smell of old tar, weathered manila, flaky rust and moist wood is overwhelming.

Foreigner summons Tom to help me stow some gear in the lazaret, and hands down some five-gallon buckets full of bolts, nuts and miscellaneous spare parts. Then come some long strips of web. With Tom in the hold and me in the lazaret, we pull what seems like miles of black tarred web. It is condensed and stuck together in a somewhat tubular form, so it seems like an anaconda of infinite length. Dust from this snake-like extremity has me gasping for air. After forty-five minutes in this noxious dungeon, I emerge sweating, choking and regurgitating lazaret pollution. It's no wonder the fishermen call the lazaret the dungeon of death.

Foreigner is standing on the deck as I emerge from the hatch. His head is tilted back as if he's eyeing something in the sky. "Hey, Raymondo," he asks, "are you afraid of heights?"

I clear my throat enough to say, "Depends." He is holding a light bulb. I follow his eyes to the top of the mast. It's a long way up, and the way to get there looks treacherous.

I look at Foreigner. "I hear you're the best mast-light changer in the fleet," I say, hoping to goad him into showing off. It didn't work.

"I just retired, you little—! In my prime I could shinny up the mast upside down and change the bulb with my toes."

I take the bulb from his hand, place the screw end between my teeth, and start up the shroud on the starb'rd side. Between the two shrouds are footholds that end about seven feet from the top of the mast. One has to reach from the uppermost foothold, barely eight inches wide, and, while hugging the mast and stretching to reach the light, remove the glass cover and hang onto it, unscrew the old bulb, screw in the new one, and replace the cover.

I move with alacrity up the lower rungs, but at twenty feet my courage weakens and my pace slows considerably. I reach the highest foothold, barely wide enough for my two feet, and embrace the mast as I would my most cherished love. Trying hard to control my fear, or at least conceal it from those eyes peering up at me from the deck, I stretch to my limit. Slowly, shakily, I remove the glass cover, cradle it under my arm, and unscrew the old bulb.

"Don't squeeze the sap outta the mast!" Foreigner yells.

Slowly, I screw the new bulb into the socket and replace the glass cover. Ah! Success! Now to get down that precarious route and plant my feet on firm deck.

"Before you come down," Foreigner yells, "let me turn on the switch and see if it works."

It works, to my vast relief. I'm sure there's a good view from up here, but I'm too scared to look. Why didn't this tub have a crow's nest, as some boats do? It would surely make this maneuver much simpler and safer.

Coming down is even harder than going up, as you have to find your footing by guess and feel, but I do get down.

"Well, Skipper, what other nice little chores do you have for me?" I ask, thinking he can't possibly top this last one.

"Glad you asked, my boy," he answers, his eyes flashing a fresh sadistic look. "Follow me."

Tom and I trail Foreigner up the ladder and along the dock, past piles of nets. Some of them are spread out over large areas of the dock, so it's necessary to walk across them. Foreigner, a few feet in front of us crosses one net, Tom and me in his wake. Suddenly the net jerks beneath our feet and the two of us are airborne. A crew inside the shed is making a pull on this particular net. Foreigner turns around in time to catch us fighting for balance.

"Put your feet on your shoulders, you knuckleheads!" he bellows. "Whenever you walk across a net, put your feet on your shoulders. That way you don't get tripped up."

Inside the net shed, Foreigner instructs Tom and me to climb to the top of the rafter beams, which are draped with the lead (pronounced "leed") net. They are six-by-twelve-inch beams about sixteen feet from the floor. The lead net is a hundred fathoms (six hundred feet) long. It is draped over three successive beams. We are to lower it to the floor.

The lead net is used for fishing close to shore in shallow water. It is dispensable, made from old web. The skipper, not wishing to risk his costly seine in shallow water, will use the lead net as the name implies—to lead the fish into the seine; the seine is linked to the lead net and laid out as the boat gets into deeper water. Fish swimming along the shore will follow the lead net into the seine.

The lead net is kept in the skiff, from which it is laid out and picked up. This is part of the skiffmen's job; there being no power assistance in the skiff, it's arm-stretching, back-breaking work.

All the heat in the net shed has risen to the ceiling, where Tom and I are working. When we finish undraping the lead, we ladder our way to floor level, wet with perspiration.

"Look, boys!" Foreigner howls to the crew. "The rafter rats are back. Give 'em a simple job and they're sweating like two stuffed pigs!"

While our faces are still dripping, Foreigner orders us to put the lead net into the skiff. I am beginning to hate the sight of that lead net.

By Friday, we have the main seine completely hung and ready to put aboard the *Emancipator*. Foreigner moves the boat opposite his shed, and the crew readies the power block to pull the seine from the shed onto the stern. Loading it takes two hours. We have to pull slowly because the seine is being dragged across the floor of the shed and across the wooden dock, where snags are numerous. A tear in the seine would require immediate repair. Once on the fishing grounds, the crew informs me, Foreigner will run the power block at high speed and the gears will scream as the seine comes storming in. He will expect the seine to be on the stern in less than thirty minutes. If it is not, his obscenities become a verbal tidal wave.

By Friday evening we are ready for the salmon season. Foreigner gives us Saturday off to rest and prepare for the opening.

4

GRIZA BOUND

ON SUNDAY THE CREW MEETS AT THE 14TH Street dock. Today we'll be leaving for the fishing grounds, a four- to five-hour run.

As I place my seabag in the fo'c'sle I hear Gene, the engineer, readying the engine. I go into the engine room and watch him start the big diesel. He just finished "oilin'," and now starts the small gas starter engine alongside the main engine. With the starter engine running, Gene pushes the lever which engages the main engine and starts it revolving. The needle of the oil-pressure gauge moves slowly into the operating zone. It's time to ignite the fuel. Gene pulls the fuel-injector lever and the dependable Caterpillar engine starts purring like a contented cat.

I listen for a moment to this mechanical masterpiece. The engine is the heart of the seining operation, expected to run sixteen to twenty hours a day for four or five months, and not miss a beat. Besides propelling the boat, it runs the winches, pumps, power block and other mechanical equipment. An engine breakdown can spell disaster to the crew, so it is crucial that it be well maintained.

Back in the fo'c'sle, all seven bunks are cluttered with seabags, oilskins, blankets, clothes and miscellaneous gear. Several pairs of black Kingfisher hip boots, a favorite with fishermen, lay on the floor. A pair of long johns and a sou'wester hang on a hook. I picture the owner wearing these out on deck some dark, rainy night, to "water the lilies." My bunk, not by choice but by lack of seniority, is on the starb'rd side. It is directly beneath the anchor winch, so the most likely to leak. It is also the closest to the line of traffic, as the ladder from the fo'c'sle to the main

deck is close by.

I go topside and my eyes pan the dock. Seine boats are tied up two abreast along its length. They're all here except for the five that have already left for the Bering Sea. Waiting quietly, as if embedded in concrete, are the seiners *Polarland, Montique, Reliance, Lemes, Point Defiance, Sunset, Solta, Cheryl Ann* and the rest of the Everett fleet. Soon they will be joining seiners from other Washington ports, to congregate in various Puget Sound locations and compete for the prized sockeye salmon.

Walking towards the stern from the fo'c'sle exit, I come to the skipper's quarters, where the pilothouse is located. Through the open doorway I notice a clutter of spare engine parts and miscellaneous gear. Eventually this paraphernalia will be stowed in a less conspicuous place.

Passing the open galley door, I peer inside. Bob, the cook, is busy putting away canned goods from boxes stacked on the table. Perishable goods are piled on every inch of flat space left in the galley. Within these mountains of groceries, Bob's head appears and disappears like a target at a carnival.

"Who's going to eat all this?" I ask. "You must have enough there for three seasons!"

"If they eat like you, this food won't last two weeks!" he answers.

I walk on to the stern. The winch has a fresh coat of dark green paint. It looks more stable now, as if the paint has strengthened it. Fresh paint covers much of the house and bulwarks, like an old woman trying to look younger by smearing on cosmetics. Nothing could make this old tub

Placid waters surround Emancipator on a set at Griza.

look young again, but she does look as if she can get through another season.

The *Emancipator* has weathered more than forty years in the tough fishing industry. She now looks rugged and dependable, but by the end of the season the seas will have washed away her makeup and she will once again spend the long winter months moored in the basin, looking weather-beaten and antiquated.

I climb the ladder to the dock, which is bustling with activity. It's departure day, always a busy time. Men scurry in all directions, doing what's necessary to get their boats ready. Here and there, small clusters of men carry on animated conversations—something about fishing, of course. Their hands and arms move to all points of the compass as they talk. It's been said that if

you tied a fisherman's hands behind his back, he would become speechless.

A diesel truck is fueling the *Polarland*. A grocery truck is unloading its cargo onto the *Lemes*. A radio technician is installing an antenna on the mast of the *Montique*. The crew of the *Pt. Defiance* is stowing the lead. I look across the dock to the long row of net sheds. Each boat has her own shed in which to stow nets and gear. Their double doors are all swung open. Over one door hangs a rusty basketball hoop, being totally ignored as the winter jocks are now crewmen on their dads' boats, or their uncles', or, like me, they're greenhorns just starting their seining careers. Gulls perch in a line along the peak of the roof, waiting for their lunchtime, which usually follows the fishermen's by a few minutes. The skiffs have

Seine boats at anchor for the evening at Langley Pt. near the Griza.

been hoisted aboard the sterns of the seiners for faster traveling. The tension and excitement are building to a climax as last-minute chores are tended to. After a full week of preparation, we're ready to sail! Friends and relatives have gathered on the dock to wish the fleet good sailing and good luck on the grounds. Crewmen are giving last-minute embraces to wives, children or girl-friends.

It is about one o'clock when Foreigner signals with several blasts of the air horn. We let go the lines and make our way slowly from the 14th Street dock. Soon a long procession of purse seiners is heading toward the jetty of Port Gardner Bay. The air is shrill with the blasts of horns. The figures on the dock, arms still waving, grow smaller and smaller. We are on our own.

Once out of the harbor the faster boats pull ahead, widening the seas between the boats. Our destination is the Griza, a Croatian word meaning a rocky cliff or bluff. Each skipper has his favorite spot, the place where he feels most confident, and he spends most of his fishing time in that place. Foreigner's spot is the Griza.

Our route will take us through Saratoga Passage, between Whidbey and Camano Islands. At the end of Whidbey we'll have to buck the strong tide through Deception Pass. Water from outer Puget Sound funnels through the small entrance at Deception Pass, only about a hundred yards wide, to fill the waterways of Skagit Bay and Saratoga Pass on each incoming tide. Of course the reverse action takes place on the outgoing tide. It's the hourglass effect.

As we travel along, hugging the shoreline of Camano, we pass beach home after beach home. We are close enough to see barbecues smoking and people enjoying a pleasant, leisurely afternoon. No leisure for us, however, as travel time is the time for the crew to do the many jobs necessary to keep a seine boat in excellent condition. A malfunction in the machinery or a breakdown in the gear can be costly. Once on the fishing grounds, everything is expected to be shipshape. Maintenance is the preoccupation of an efficient crew.

Usually a skipper will plan to run Deception Pass at slack time, when for a few minutes the turbulent water is comparatively serene. Not our skipper; we'll be running the pass on a strong tide. I haven't been through the pass before, though I know its reputation for treachery. As we approach, I go to the pilothouse to look at the navigation chart. Foreigner has gone to the flying bridge to steer. From there he has a 360-degree view, and he needs it because of boat traffic and other hazards.

From the pilothouse I see the narrow entrance to the pass. An arched bridge spans the gap. Water around the boat begins to boil, though we're still half a mile away. At one spot just inside the bridge, the water rushes past a rock outcropping which creates an eddy. The water is two feet higher on one side of the rock than the other, creating an impressive overflow.

I climb topside and watch Foreigner maneuver through the narrow, steep-walled gap. He sees me and yells, "Tell the cook to make sure the dishes are secure."

I rush down the ladder, stick my head into the galley, and give Bob the message.

"Tell the skipper I've got roast beef in the oven, and if he wants dinner tonight, he'd better keep this tub steady!" Bob bellows, so loudly that I don't need to relay the message to the skipper.

Suddenly, the boat lurches to port at an alarming angle. Dishes rattle in their cubbyholes. The coffeepot slides across the top of the stove and crashes into the railing around the perimeter of the stove (there to keep the cooking utensils from sliding onto the floor in just such a situation as this). Coffee spurts from the spout of the pot and sizzles on the hot surface, sending up a small cloud of steam. The roasting pan is banging against the oven walls. Bob is reaching in all directions, trying to control the galley goods and at the same time control his own balance. He looks like W.C. Fields trying to save the gin bottles on his bar during a violent earthquake.

"Tell the skipper if he wants hash for dinner tonight, just keep this up!" Bob roars.

Now the boat lurches sharply to starb'rd, and everything loose in the galley starts a return trip. The strong tides and whirlpools that flow through Deception Pass toss the largest seine boats around like toys.

I make my way carefully back to the bridge. The rest of the crew, wallowing in the stern, is clinging to whatever can keep them upright. I hear Paul yell, "Yahoo!" Paul loves rough seas. On the bridge, Foreigner turns the wheel hard in one direction, then in the opposite direction, changing course so fast and frequently, our wake is a foaming seesaw. The water around our hull is churning in so many directions it's hard to tell which way the tide is running. Everywhere there are whirlpools big enough to swallow a man. A large piece of driftwood, caught in a whirlpool, disappears in a second, like a cigarette stub flushed down a toilet. Finally, we reach a point where things stabilize.

We follow the shoreline another few miles, then drop anchor in a small bay, having first launched the skiff off the stern. It's easier to launch the skiff while the boat is in motion. Several other boats are anchored in the bay. A wind from the south carries threatening clouds, though no rain has fallen. In the lee of the point, we should be protected from any seas that may develop during the night. As soon as the anchor is secure, Foreigner orders Gene to cut the engine. How quiet it seems, after hours of the noise and vibration of the diesel!

The crew assembles near the hatch for what is to be my first course in "basic scuttlebutt," also known as B.S. time. Bob is in the galley,

Foreigner (Nick) at the wheel, about to enter notorious Deception Pass.

busy with meal preparations. He can work more efficiently now that stability prevails. We joke and make small talk while we wait for Bob to make up for lost time. The fresh sea air has a way of stimulating the appetite, and though we chat, I'm sure food is uppermost in all our minds.

The skippers of the several other boats at anchor shout back and forth to one another. They catch up on what's been going on since last season. It's a reunion every year at this time—the same boats and the same skippers. The crewmen know that when two seine boats come alongside each other, the skippers do most of the talking. The crews, like spectators, are expected to stand around and listen as the skippers exchange information, an occasional quip, or some humorous anecdote.

There is one exception: the *St. Nicholas*, which is anchored near us. Her skipper, Paul, a good friend of Foreigner's, is comparatively reserved. No sooner have the two skippers started a conversation than a loud, belligerent lout aboard the *St. Nicholas* cuts in on Paul. Every time Paul opens his mouth, this loony cuts in with a raucous stream of oral oddities. It seems this man has been with Paul for a number of years, and Paul accepts his compulsion to dominate.

Paul, a top fisherman at the Griza, has the respect of all the other skippers who fish this area. Foreigner admits to having learned to fish the Griza from Paul.

A moderate wind is blowing from the southwest, and the boat is pulling persistently against her anchor line. It will take us a few days to get

17

our sea legs under us.

Bob calls us to dinner. We make haste for the galley, where the smell of roast beef prevails. I take my seat in the far corner, followed by Tom, Nels, Sam, Paul and Foreigner. We have to enter in that order, and once inside the five of us are locked in until dinner is finished. Bob and Gene have freedom on the other side of the table.

The cookstove has been going all day, and the galley is hot. The door and two small windows don't admit enough air to cool even this small room. Anyone who suffers from claustrophobia certainly would not enjoy a meal here.

Foreigner takes his place at the head of the table. "Well, boys," he says, "enjoy your meal, the practice is over. Tomorrow we go into the stadium and play the game. We gotta win this one for the Gipper." (Foreigner is an avid Notre Dame fan.)

"To hell with the Gipper," Gene says. "Let's win this one for us!"

Foreigner takes off his soiled hat and whacks Gene's curly locks. "You little bastard!" he howls, in a display of anger that may be serious or may be play-acting. I am not sure which.

Nels smiles. Paul chuckles. The cook cracks up with a robust roar. It doesn't take much to activate his funny bone, and when he laughs, the whole boat shakes.

Foreigner, now looking rational, looks at the sumptuous roast in the center of the table and says, "Who's going to pay for this gourmet grub? We haven't made a cent yet, and we're eating like royalty!"

"We earned it," Tom remarks jokingly. "We worked all last week for free."

"You call that work?" Foreigner exclaims. "That was play. Tomorrow you'll find out what work is!"

"You guys can talk all night," Sam interrupts. "I'm going to have some of this roast." Food for talk is his motto.

"Me too!" Paul declares, raising his wine glass overhead.

We all raise our glasses, then swallow their contents. Foreigner refills his glass from the gallon jug of Tavallo nearby. Wine is a staple on these Croat boats. It's not unusual for a crew to go through a gallon in one meal.

Paul, the old salt, sits next to Foreigner. He's wearing a mischievous expression, as usual, as if he is always on the verge of coming out with some witticism. His lips twitch while his mind is formulating some salty satire, and the crew appreciates his sense of humor. Paul is a very likable fellow.

"Easy for you," he says. "Roast beef, potatoes, corn, salad, dessert—a meal fit for a king. Now, back when I started fishing, all we got was stale pilot bread and maybe a piece of salt codfish if we were lucky. Furthermore, if anyone complained he got flogged with the cat-o-nine-tails. If that didn't cure him, he was keelhauled—not once, but keelhauled until he turned blue. Next, he was ordered to the top of the mast with only his skivvies on. Several hours later, just before he froze to death, the skipper would order him down and say, 'A day or two in the lazaret without any grub ought to straighten you out.' And you mama's boys think you have it tough!" Paul concludes with a chuckle.

"The B.S. is getting so deep in here," Gene says, "I'm going to have to put on my boots."

"While you're down there," Bob says, "how about you bring me up one of those Playboy magazines you've got stashed under your mattress?"

"My private reserve," Gene responds. "Nobody gets those!"

Bob roars with laughter that shakes his whole body.

Foreigner takes off his cap and whacks Gene on the head. "That's for bringing those dirty books aboard," he growls.

Gene fends off the attack with his arm, then says haughtily, "What I do with my spare time is my own damn business."

Foreigner looks him straight in the eye and retorts, "From this moment on, my friend, you aren't going to have any spare time. For starters, get down in the engine room and grease all the fittings on the engine, the power take-off, the winch and the propeller shaft. Then clean and polish the engine. I want to be able to eat off that engine."

Gene gets up, grabs the coffeepot from the top of the stove, fills his ever-in-hand mug, and then ladders down to the engine room.

"Another glass of wine for everyone," Foreigner announces. Again we all raise our glasses. "Well, tell me Raymondo," Foreigner continues, eyeing me, "what do you think of this business?"

"One thing is for sure, the food is better than on a gillnetter," I answer with a lingering look at the bare bone in the roasting pan.

"Sure it is," Foreigner agrees, "but there's a price you hafta pay. Dishpan hands. It's the skiffman's job to do the dinner dishes."

I look with dismay at all the dirty dishes on the table and in the sink, and suggest we use paper plates.

"Paper plates, my butt!" Foreigner bellows. "You think this is a picnic?"

The antiquated galley has an old-style hand pump with a spout that flows into the sink. The water has to be heated on the stove, then poured into the sink. It's a small sink, inadequate for the job. The dishes are rinsed in a large pan. All in all, doing the dishes is quite a chore, and I think the cook has dirtied every dish and utensil in the galley. What's more, I'll bet he's laughing about it now, out on the stern with the crew. To make things worse, the sink is right next to the hot stove. "I thought they'd abolished slavery back in the 1800s!" I grumble to myself.

Meanwhile, Foreigner and the crew are making final inspections of the seine and the mechanical apparatus, to make sure everything is ready for tomorrow morning. Tom has gone over the skiff to make sure it's ready for action. The seine skiff is not the small rowboat usually referred to as a skiff. This is a fifteen-foot craft, heavily built and designed for rugged use. Its engine, two hundred horsepower or more, may be gas or diesel. It turns a propeller nearly as large as the prop on the mother boat. It can pull like a tug. A good, powerful skiff has saved many a skipper his seine or his boat.

Foreigner calls me to the stern and gives me last-minute instructions about the skiff, then says that Tom will show me the ropes during the initial set. Everything about the seine seems complicated to me at this point. Lines, web, purse rings, corks, leads—what kept them from getting tangled?

It requires a lot of hard work, knowledge and coordination of crew to successfully operate a large fishing boat and seine. The skipper must have a lot of experience as many conditions must be given consideration: the speed of the fish and the direction they are traveling must be estimated; the speed, direction and stage of tide; wind velocity and direction; how far ahead of the swimming salmon the seine must be laid; the effect of other boats and seines in the immediate area, plus a multitude of other factors.

Before long it is dark and the crew has hit the bunks. The other boats, where crews were shouting and laughing, are quiet now. The mast lights, high above each boat, shine like guardian angels over the anchored fleet. Skippers are lying in their bunks, mentally mapping their strategies for tomorrow. Crewmen are dreaming of a bonanza—the Big Run.

I have a hard time falling asleep. I lie there listening to the squeaks and groans as the *Emancipator* pitches up and down on the gentle waves. From just outside, through the thickness of the planking, I hear the water sloshing against the hull. In the bunk below me, Bob has already started his infamous snoring. From under someone's blankets comes a flatulent sound, then a faint chuckle. From the other side of the fo'c'sle comes the faint murmur of a voice—someone talking in his sleep. I lie there for some time, hearing the unfamiliar sounds of the boat and her crew.

I have just fallen asleep, or so it seems, when the irritating ring of an alarm clock wakes me. Through the cobwebs in my mind I hear the sounds of someone fumbling in the darkness for clothes. Then a light goes on, blinding me for the moment. What the hell is this character doing in the middle of the night, I wonder.

Nels waits for orders from skipper to release pelican hook, which will initiate a set.

"What's going on?" I mumble.

"What's going on? Fishing! That's what's going on," replies the fumbling figure. It's Bob, the cook.

"What time is it?" I ask.

"Three-fifteen," he says, slipping on a shoe.

"Oh, my God!" I groan.

"The season opens in forty-five minutes," he says as he starts toward the galley.

He must be kidding, I think, so I reach up

and pull on the ceiling light, turning off the light, then close my eyes. My mind is afloat. Ah, this bunk feels so good now. It's starting to shape itself to my body. Nice. My conscious mind is opening the door for my subconscious.

Suddenly I hear a pounding on the deck above my bunk. It sounds as though a herd of buffalo is stampeding just above my head. What the hell . . . ? I'm about to dismiss it all as a bad dream when Foreigner's voice comes booming down the fo'c'sle companionway. "Okay, you misfits! Both feet on deck! Let's move it!"

The light switches on again. Bodies emerge from cubbyholes like bees from a honeycomb. Six men, trying to dress hurriedly in an area not much larger than a phone booth, struggling with long johns, pants, hip boots and the rest seems a little absurd.

To some it's just another day in a fisherman's life. Paul, as if he had been up for hours, sings joyfully as he dresses, "Oh, it's a sailor's life for me! You take the land and I'll take the sea!"

Everyone else is dressed and out of the fo'c'sle in minutes. I dress groggily and make my way topside. It's still dark and a fresh wind is rattling the rigging. The aroma of fresh-brewed coffee wafts from the galley door.

Foreigner and the crew fill the galley. As I enter, Foreigner proclaims, "Well! Raise the flag! Raymondo is up!"

"This is a helluva time to wake a man," I grumble.

"That might be the most sleep you'll get all season," he snaps back. "From now to September you'll forget what a good night's sleep was like."

Seen through hazy eyes, Foreigner's blurred image is like an apparition of Lucifer and, to this groggy greenhorn, his guttural voice does nothing to enhance the mood of the morning.

The cook pours a cup of coffee and places it in front of me. "Here," he says. "This will clear away some of the cobwebs."

Foreigner eyes me intently. "Are you a good sailor?" he asks. "By the look of things, you'll be bouncing around like a cork today."

"I guess I'll find out today," I answer. "Do you have stabilizers on the skiff?"

"Stabilizers? Hell, no! You think this is a yachting party? You're gonna suffer, my boy, suffer like every skiffman does." He gulps the last of his coffee, then says, "Come with me, Raymondo. I've got a job for you."

I follow him up to the bow. We stop at the anchor winch.

"I'm going to show you how to operate this," he says. "It'll be your job every morning to raise the anchor."

The winch is a mechanical type, run off a shaft from the main engine. It has two levers, a clutch and a brake. As Foreigner winds in the cable I see that it also takes manual coordination. The last fifteen or twenty feet are heavy chain with four-inch links. When the chain starts winding around the drum, it's necessary to push or pull on the incoming chain to keep an even spool. A little carelessness, and a hand can get wrapped up in the chain. When the anchor comes up, it's important to take the winch out of gear at the precise instant the anchor hits the bow saddle, or all hell breaks loose.

"You get the picture?" Foreigner asks over his shoulder as he leaves.

"I think so . . . ."

By now the crew has assembled in the galley for a mug-up, and Foreigner has the boat headed for the fishing grounds. The cook has made oven toast. This is all we'll get until some time in the morning when there's a gap in the fishing operation and we can squeeze in breakfast.

When we enter the open water of Rosario Strait, away from the protection of the point, our bow begins rising and lowering with agonizing regularity. When she reaches the apex of a wave and drops into the trough, the *Emancipator* jerks and everything that can shift its position does.

Like Paul, Bob is undaunted by the rough weather. "Sounds like the skiff is banging against the stern. We're in for a doozy, boys." Do I detect a gleam of sadism in his goggle eyes?

Paul, grinning in anticipation, tells us, "Nothing like getting your sea stomach and legs the first day out."

"I'd rather work into it gradually," Gene says dolefully.

All of us, holding our mugs to keep the coffee from spilling, brace ourselves to compensate for the boat's tossing.

Tom looks at his watch. "Well, Ray," he says, "I guess we'd better get into the skiff. It's a quarter to four."

The first day of fishing is like the first day of practice for a football team. It takes a while to get organized, iron out the rough spots, and start working as a team. Each has a specific job to perform. Each man must learn his function, so the crew becomes a well-coordinated unit. As I'm the only crewmember with no seining experience, we'll have an easier time developing coordination than would a crew with several greenhorns.

Tom and I put on our foul-weather gear, hurry to the stern, and climb into the skiff. The skiff is bouncing erratically against the stern, so we have some difficulty boarding. Tom has thrown the seine line into the skiff and, with a wooden pin used as a steadfast, makes this line secure to the bow of the skiff. Seine and skiff are now attached and ready for action. Tom starts the diesel engine.

The water looks black as coal. The overcast sky still shrouds us in darkness. The *Emancipator* has slowed her speed. Now she idles around what appears to be a small rock islet. The mast lights of six other boats are visible close by, jockeying for position while awaiting the opening gun.

The skiff is rocking up and down with such force that it seems the line to the main boat is likely to snap. Holding on for dear life, like a couple of rancheros breaking broncos, Tom and I ride this angry stallion. I feel the first signs of nausea. This agitated sea is disrupting my self-confidence, if I had any, as a seaman. Fumes from the skiff's exhaust add to my discomfort.

From the bridge, unseen in the darkness, Foreigner yells "MOLA!" Then comes the clang as the pelican hook is released. The skiff jerks, dips, and moves slowly away from the stern of the mother boat.

"Pull the pin!" Tom screams.

I fumble at the wooden pin near the bow that holds the towline. When this pin is pulled, it frees the skiff to turn 180 degrees and tow the seine.

"Pull the pin!" Tom screams again, louder.

The skiff, throttling fast in reverse, is putting tremendous pressure on the towline and the pin. I pull and jerk at the pin with all my might, but it is not about to surrender.

"Pull it out!" comes a panicked plea from Tom.

I pull until I'm blue in the face, and then I pull harder. The pin still doesn't budge. Bracing my foot against the side of the skiff, I strain with all my weight. Tom eases the throttle. The pin comes out as if greased. I crash against the opposite side of the skiff, pin in hand. The skiff quickly turns 180 degrees, and Tom rams full throttle ahead. The towline swings around to the stern and soon it's taut as a banjo string.

The seine comes slipping off the stern of the *Emancipator*, into the dark depths of the water. Before long the *Emancipator* fades away in the darkness, only her faint mast light a clue to her whereabouts. From not far away come the sounds of a seine coming off the stern of another boat.

We're in our first set, or haul. The mother boat is towing one end of the seine and we, a quarter of a mile away, are towing the other end. The seine is supposed to assume the shape of a semicircle, but in this obscure setting—who knows? The skipper is now directing the act by instinct. When—if—the fish swim into the seine, the two boats will tow for each other to close the escape route.

Foreigner signals Tom with a flashlight. Tom answers with another, while the greenhorn in the bow of the skiff fights to repel the seasickness pervading his body. His stomach, already approaching his larynx, warns of the soon-to-be eruption.

We have towed for about fifteen minutes when Foreigner gives the signal to close. Tom turns to starb'rd. The skiff leans into the turn. The noise of the engine is deafening as Tom increases to full throttle. We are closing the circle. A faint hint of daylight is now peering over the high hills of the Griza, and the silhouette of the mother boat is more distinct.

I try to control my seasickness, as I have duties to perform. When we're within range, I must throw the seine line to someone who'll be waiting in the bow of the mother boat. This I am expected to do successfully on the first throw. If I don't, it takes precious time to recoil the line and heave it again. I have the coiled line ready as we approach.

"Let 'er go!" yells the man on the bow.

Foreigner yells "Let 'er go" to start a set."

Start of set, skiff pulls seine from mother boat. The skiff will turn 180% and tow the end of seine.

I let go with a forceful heave. The line, uncoiling as it soars high in the air, looks to be headed in the right direction. The wind-up, the delivery and the follow-through are correct, but before I can congratulate myself, a gust of wind catches the exposed line and blows it away from the outstretched arms of the intended receiver. Back comes the line like tangled spaghetti. Foreigner hollers obscenities at me from the bridge, with such intensity that it may have flickered the flame of the Smith Island Lighthouse. Should anyone have been waiting to savor the serenity and beauty of the dawn from the Deception Pass Bridge, he surely would have retreated from the bellowed blasphemies rising from the darkness.

With misery in my midriff and distress in my psyche, I recoil the line and ready for another throw. Tom maneuvers closer. I let fly again. No profanity from the bridge. Tom releases the line from the skiff's tow bit and makes a hasty run to the starb'rd side of the mother boat. I jump aboard and wait on deck for instructions from Foreigner.

The deck area, illuminated now by a floodlight mounted on the mast, looks confusing to me. Six men are scurrying around, pulling in various lines.

"Pull up the breast line!" Foreigner yells at me.

"What the hell's the breast line?" I ask, looking frantically around at the multitude of lines.

"Here," Foreigner pants. "Untie this line and put it on the niggerhead."

"Niggerhead?"

"The winch, *boozdoe!*"

The two purse lines are already on the main spool of the winch. Nels is pulling on one and Sam on the other. Both are making neat coils of line on the deck. I try, with all the skill of a greenhorn, to carry out Foreigner's orders. The breast line promptly tangles around the niggerhead. Bob pushes the lever to stop the winch.

"Don't stop that winch!" Foreigner bellows.

"This line's screwed up!" I yell, pulling frantically, trying to free the line.

"You never stop the winch unless it's an emergency!" Foreigner screams.

"What do you call this?" I ask.

"Stupidity, that's what! Anyone who can't do a simple job like that is a knucklehead!"

Bob helps me untangle the line, then quickly restarts the winch. With extreme caution I pull the line through the revolving niggerhead. More than anything else I want to halt those scornful blasts from the skipper. I manage to raise and secure the breast line. Vastly relieved and pleased with my success, I stand by the winch to catch my breath.

Foreigner again: "What the hell are you? A statue? Didn't anyone ever tell you that anything with one breast has two of 'em? Get your butt over there and pull up that other breast line!"

The two purse lines, running through separate davits, one on each side of the winch, are between the other breast line and me. Both are taut as bow strings and dripping salt water as they come reeling in. Either of those lines could saw a man in two. I crawl under them on my hands and knees. Anxiously, cautiously, I raise and secure the other breast line.

Dawn is now lighting the work area, and my seasickness has abated, temporarily, under the scorn of the skipper and pressure of unrehearsed performance.

Foreigner, now in Dr. Jekyll mode, takes a position aside the port gun'nel. He hums a tune and plunges a pole rhythmically into the water.

It is a straight pole, probably alder, about fifteen feet long, with an inverted bowl-like object affixed to one end—same principle as the household gadget called a plumber's friend or toilet plunger. This plunger, when pushed forcefully into the water, produces a stream of bubbles that scare the fish and prevent them from escaping through the opening between the two ends of the seine. Not until the seine is completely pursed will their escape be impossible.

Plunging is the skipper's job. It is a fine art, and each skipper has his own technique. Foreigner's style is to raise the long, flexible pole out of the water and then, using the gun'nel for leverage, spring the pole high into the air. When the bowl at the end has reached its apex, he drives it down deep into the water.

"Bubbles, bubbles, my boys!" Foreigner sings merrily after each dramatic plunge. He is really enjoying himself. It may be that plunging serves him as a pacifier. While he is springing and popping the plunger his eyes are scanning the operation. Many things can go wrong—tide, wind, currents, mechanics, debris in the water, interference from other boats and other seines. Plunging and singing may very well be his way of relieving tension. POP! Goes the plunger. "Singin' in the rain, just singin' in the rain, what a glorious . . . ."

Suddenly he is back in his Mr. Hyde mode. "Raymondo! Gene! Pull! Pull that web from the purse line! Quick! You two move like a pair of turtles! You need a hot poker to your *gazitzas* to get you to move!"

Gene and I pull at the web, which the tide is carrying over the incoming purse line. Bending over the rail and reaching down, we pull frantically, straining our guts.

"Pull hard and it'll come easy!" Foreigner assures us.

It is arm-straining, back-breaking work, but after several agonizing minutes the web finally clears the purse line. I flex my back and pray that this is not normal procedure.

Down goes the plunger. "Bubbles, my boys! Bubbles! Tra . . . la . . . la . . . ."

When the seine is pursed up, Paul, Nels, Gene, Sam and I assemble on the stern to pick up. Bob operates the lever which controls the power block, and Foreigner watches from the deck to clear any tangles before the seine goes through the power block, located overhead on the boom. The seine comes in dripping wet and we're working under it, so we put on our rain gear. The seine must be piled neatly on the stern, so it won't tangle when it is laid out on the next set. Nels piles the cork line. Gene piles the lead line. Paul, Sam and I pile the web.

The wind, out of the southwest, has grown stronger, and rain slashes our faces. Swells rock the boat and the crew struggles for balance. It's not the sort of weather we expect at the beginning of summer. While I'm bouncing around on the stern my stomach keeps reminding me that it is not happy. I'm hoping to hold back the sickness until the seine is aboard, and I may be free to find an isolated place where I can unload my misery. Letting fly now would be humiliating.

Foreigner again, firing instructions at us: "Nels, make a nice cork pile! Gene, keep that lead line clear! The rest of you, pile that web nice and neat! I'm going to take a picture of this pile afterwards."

Then he turns and waves his arm in a circular motion. Tom, in the skiff tethered at the end of the tow line, speeds up the engine. Tom's job is to keep the mother boat from engaging with the seine. While the seine is being picked up, the floating corks and web can get tangled in the prop and rudder.

It seems like a long, long time, but finally the seine is aboard. The skipper had the power block slowed down on this initial set, but that will change. From now on, it'll be, "Damn the torpedoes! Full speed ahead!"

In the bundt at the end of the seine, about a dozen sockeyes are splashing desperately, trying to escape.

"Well, boys, we really killed 'em this time!" Foreigner laments. "It may pay for breakfast if you guys don't eat too much."

The tide has carried us some distance. After we tie the skiff to the stern, Foreigner heads the boat back toward the towhead (starting point). "Feed the skiffmen breakfast," he instructs the cook.

As Tom and I enter the galley, the misery in my stomach is about to blow the cork. How sick must you be before you die? Death must surely be more comfortable than this.

Bob is busy trying to coordinate his movements in the rolling galley. "How are you boys doing out in the canoe?" he asks.

"Okay," says Tom, "but I don't think Ray is feeling so good."

"Sorry to hear that!" Bob says, malice dripping from every word. "What he needs is some of this juicy bacon. Like this . . . " and he holds up a slice with the fat dripping freely from it.

I dash for the galley door and run into Paul, who is about to enter. I rush to the stern, hoping to reach the skiff in time. I don't—I fall on my knees behind the seine pile and heave into the angry sea. It feels as if everything inside of me is abandoning me in favor of Davey Jones. As I kneel there peering down at the dark, ominous sea, I get a mental picture of Dad's fish market. Somehow pawing through ice, cleaning crabs and slicing fish seem like pleasant pastimes.

Allowing no time for recuperation, we make three more hauls without much success. Then, thank goodness, Foreigner decides it isn't worth the wear on the gear in such unfavorable seas. We anchor in the same bay as the night before. At dinner I'm the target for rapid verbal fire from the crew. Hardy seamen seem to relish seeing a greenhorn suffer. I absorb their ridicule through dinner and the dishwashing, then retreat to the afterdeck. There I find solace and renew some of my self-respect. By the time I enter the fo'c'sle my disposition has improved considerably.

However, not for long. I crawl into my bunk with thoughts of a restful night after my inaugural day of purse seining. I assume a comfortable position facing the deck beam, only twelve inches above my head. The paint on the beam is blistered and cracked, and a dark, rusty stain streaks its

The skipper doing his favorite job – plunging. "Bubbles, my boys, bubbles."

surface. A globule of liquid forms on the bottom of the beam as I watch. It lengthens into a pear shape and hangs there, clinging to the beam, its stem stretching slowly. The globule hangs there for a few seconds, then falls onto my forehead. It trickles down the side of my face and onto the pillow. My "choice" bunk has fulfilled its promise.

Next morning we are awakened at the same ungodly hour. The seas have calmed, but the rain is still falling drearily. The crew dresses and makes for the warmth and shelter of the

galley while I rush to the bow to raise the anchor as the skipper had instructed me on opening day. Foreigner, having raised the anchor hundreds of times, made it look easy. By showing me one time, he thinks he's taught me to master it. This is my first raising and I feel very apprehensive.

Releasing the brake lever, I pull back on the clutch lever, which starts the cable winding around the drum of the winch. As the cable winds, it's necessary to push or pull on it to keep an even spool, being extra cautious not to get a hand wrapped in the drum. No time to think about girls here—it's one hundred percent attention on the drum. After winding several fathoms of cable, a link comes through the bow saddle which joins the cable to the anchor chain. This means only a few more fathoms before the anchor breaks the water.

Now I'm really getting nervous, remembering how crucial it is to brake and clutch correctly the instant the anchor hits the bow saddle. With wild anticipation I wait for the anchor . . . there it is! Quickly I ease the clutch to slow its advance through the bow saddle, but the U-bolt of the anchor hangs up on the saddle. Additional clutch must be given—more clutch—still more clutch—the anchor comes charging through the bow saddle like a deranged Doberman. It bashes forcefully against the bow saddle with a loud metallic clank; the sudden jolt reverberates through the whole boat and resounds loudly within the surrounding bay. Frozen with fright, I stand motionless as the chain tightens and the anchor pulls forcefully at the bow saddle as if to tear it from the bow. Gears whine and scream, the clamor of metal against metal, and the boat shutters violently.

Foreigner comes charging to the bow, pushes me aside, tightens the brake wheel and throws the clutch lever off.

"What the hell you trying to do?" he screams. "Tear the boat apart?"

Apparently my quick course in Basic Anchor Raising 101 was not sufficient. I retreat to the galley.

The coffee and oven toast taste exceptionally good this damp, dark morning, and the galley assumes a degree of coziness. Sheltered from the weather, enjoying the warmth from the stove, one can easily become mesmerized by such comfort. It's a chance for some leisure moments before the hectic pace once fishing starts.

Foreigner has gone to the bridge now and is steering towards the fishing grounds. Outside, the mast lights of half a dozen boats move slowly southward, like bright stars in the obscured sky. The sea is both awesome and mysterious in the vast darkness. Only dawn can dissolve the unfamiliar ambience that surrounds the boat.

Below the galley, the mighty Caterpillar hums its rhythmic beat, and the vibration works the galley floor, massaging the feet like an electric vibrator designed for that purpose. The aroma from the coffeepot and the mellow voices of morning are soothing to the soul. A stay here can easily spoil a crew.

Not this morning, though. Gene, sitting close to the stove, begins coughing. After several coughs in rapid succession, he grabs his mug and bursts out the door. Then Paul and Sam begin competing in a choking frenzy. Nels, trying to control his gag reflex, puts his hand to his mouth. Tom and I, locked in the corner, begin barking like a couple of excited dogs. The next moment the crew is gasping for breath and fighting for the exit.

My first thought is that some toxic fumes have escaped the engine room. I dismiss this idea as soon as I reach the afterdeck. Bob, his white cook's hat clutched in a fist, is roaring and shaking with laughter. It's new to me, this "pepper on the stove" routine, but it has been a tradition among the sadistic culinary virtuosos.

We make four sets at the Griza without inflating our pocketbooks. Shortly before noon, we head across Rosario Strait. According to the scuttlebutt, we are heading for Iceberg Point, on the southern tip of Lopez Island.

Foreigner calls me to the bridge. He points to a landmark on Lopez, a few miles away, and tells me to steer for it. " 'Bout an hour's run," he tells me, then joins the rest of the crew for lunch in the galley.

While I'm steering I recall an excerpt from Mark Twain's *Life on the Mississippi,* and I wonder whether, as in the book, Foreigner and the crew are setting me up for some chicanery. In this incident, young Sam Clemens is an apprentice river pilot under the tutorship of a master pilot of the highest order. The master pilot always stayed in the pilothouse while Clemens took his turn at the wheel. After being tutored for a few weeks, Clemens began to get a little cocky and thought he knew the river as well as the master did. Wishing to bring the young apprentice back to reality, the pilot devised a plan. One day, as they were approaching what looked like troubled water, he slipped quietly out the back door of the pilothouse.

When the riverboat neared the apparent calamity, young Clemens became increasingly agitated. He held his tongue until, directly in front of the bow, he could see every indication of shallow water over a sandbar. Now near panic, he screamed, "Sir, is that a sandbar?" Silence. Again he screamed his question. Still no answer. He turned and saw that the pilot was not in the room. In desperation he signaled the engine room for full speed astern. The boat came to a full stop in midstream.

At this point the master pilot walked casually to the bow, looked up to the pilothouse, and said, "Why are you stopping, my boy? We have a schedule to meet. Please proceed."

Many of the passengers, catching onto the ploy, strolled to the bow, looked up at the embarrassed apprentice, and snickered. It was an effective cure for a know-it-all novice.

When we reach Iceberg, Tom and I crawl into the skiff. There are about thirty boats milling around, most of them close to the rocky shoreline. Foreigner maneuvers the *Emancipator*, trying to jockey her into a position favorable for a set.

"Mola lead!" he yells from the bridge, making a raised arm motion.

Tom throws a box into the water. It looks like a wooden soda-pop case, but it has another purpose here. As soon as it hits the water, it starts pulling the lead net from the stern of the skiff. We move rapidly across the surface of the water, the lead net flying out from our stern. In a few short minutes the entire lead is in the water and Tom yells, "Mola!" Nels hears the command and pulls a short line connected to the pelican hook. This releases the seine, which starts flowing off the stern of the mother boat. In less than ten minutes we have nearly a half mile of net in the water, a combination of lead and seine. Together they form a huge semicircle stretching out from shore.

Plunging is necessary here, as there's a gap under the skiff between the lead and the seine. A six-foot plunger is kept in the skiff, and I get to practice plunging. With only a six-foot pole, I can't hope to achieve the elegance with which Foreigner executes this maneuver. The idea is that fish swimming along the shore will hit the lead, then, if they're scared away from the gap between lead and seine, they enter the seine. Salmon tend to swim away from shore when encountering an obstruction.

While we wait for the mother boat to close the circle of the seine, Tom turns off our engine. This reduces the danger of getting the lead net tangled in our propeller—a mishap that can enrage any skipper, even one with the mildest disposition.

The rain forces Tom and me to put on foul-weather gear. Here we sit, like two ostracized gulls on a drifting log, waiting for the mother boat to bring the seine around in a complete circle. Another boat has laid out in front of us, and I wonder how we expect to catch any fish with that fence there.

"Get ready with the throw line," Tom instructs me after a tow of about twenty minutes. The *Emancipator* is approaching the skiff. When her bow is about ten feet from us, I let the line fly. It uncoils and Nels catches it. Perfecto! My aim is getting better. I expect a word of commendation from the skipper on the bridge, but no. Instead he pulls the cigar out of his mouth and shouts, "Okay, you bastards, don't take all day to pick up that lead. I'll hang you both from the mast if I don't see smoke coming from the roller!"

The roller he refers to is a free-rolling type on the stern of the skiff. No power here—just the muscles of the skiffmen. The lead net is picked up over the roller, so the faster the skiffmen pick up the lead, the faster the roller spins. Tom and I leap to the stern and begin pulling in the heavy, water-laden net. This lead net, made from some old cotton web of uncertain vintage, soaks up water like a sponge and it's as heavy as a waterlogged mattress.

We pull until our arms ache, and inevitably I think

of Foreigner's oft-repeated, "Pull hard and it'll come easy!" Steamy perspiration begins to accumulate inside our oilskins. The speed of the spinning roller has slowed considerably. Tom is pulling the cork line and some web, while I pull the lead line and the remainder of the web. If one of us lags behind, it shows in the web. The one who's behind has to pick up the slack so he doesn't lose face with his partner. There's no room for a freeloader in this two-man team.

There's a hard and fast rule that the skiffmen are expected to follow: pick up the lead and return to the mother boat by the time the seine is pursed—about fifteen minutes. After we get the lead aboard, Tom full-throttles the skiff toward the mother boat, which has drifted away from us. Once alongside, I jump aboard. Tom takes off with the towline, to tow the mother boat and keep her from engaging with the seine. The crew is just lowering the rings on the deck.

Paul drilling the greenhorn on clever "comebacks" for Foreigner. Double-block, in background, raises tow line to enable boat to maneuver.

Foreigner strikes again, "What the hell were you two doing out there? Dreaming about girls?"

"We picked up 'til we were blue in the face," I reply, thinking to impress him by repeating one of his favorite sayings.

Foreigner is not impressed. "Like hell!" he barks. "The only thing blue on you is gonna be your butt if you don't start movin' it!"

I jump to the stern and join Sam and Paul to pile the web. Paul kids me about Foreigner's verbal onslaught. "Don't take ____ from him," he tells me. Back on the stern, away from Foreigner's

ears, he drills me on clever comebacks to use in retaliation. Most likely I'll never use any of them. I don't like the idea of hanging upside down from the mast.

We pick up the seine and have about forty sockeyes, our best haul so far. On the current market each fish is worth about $1.60. At least we're paying our expenses.

That evening, after the dinner dishes are washed and tucked away, Bob pulls a checkerboard out from under the galley seat. I have learned through others in the crew that Bob is an expert checker-player, possibly the best in the fleet. Without apparent effort he defeats

30

Gene, Tom and Paul in turn. Now it's up to me. Having watched him play, I decide that it's best to take an offensive approach—attack and apply unrelenting pressure.

"I'll show you how it's done," I say confidently as I take my place opposite Bob.

"Oh, sure!" Foreigner taunts. "I'll give you about as much chance as Liberace in the ring with Joe Louis!"

Paul, sitting next to me, says "Nobody beat him all last season. He's the champ."

"He's unbeatable," Tom affirms.

I launch my attack. I have to ponder every move, while Bob moves almost before I get my fingers off my checker. Every time I jump one of his men, he jumps two or three of mine. The game ends just as the rest expected, with half of Bob's checkers still on the board.

The first few days of the season are relatively slow, so the crew has some leisure moments now and then. The pace picks up as the season progresses, and leisure moments are mostly memories.

We spend the rest of the week fishing the Griza and Iceberg Point. Our Griza sets start from an islet just offshore. The tide carries the seine and the boat alongside a steep cliff, where the water depth plunges straight down from the rock bluff. Before each set, Foreigner instructs Tom, "Hold 'er tight to the rocks!" Tom tows the end of the seine so close to the rocks that they almost scrape the skiff's bottom.

The islet from which we start each set is called the towhead. Here boats must wait their turns. The wait can range from a few minutes to an hour or more, depending upon the number of boats competing for turns. Normally, out of courtesy and custom, the second boat in line gives the first boat a twenty minute show. That means twenty minutes for the seine to drift away from the towhead before the next boat comes in and blocks access to the first seine. Occasionally a boat, over-anxious or just greedy, will set out of turn. This inevitably causes flared tempers on the victimized boat. The boat doing the corking will deliberately set in front of the other boat, and block off access to the seine—in other words, cork the seine so the salmon, if any, can't enter it.

On the runs from the Griza to Iceberg the cook serves a meal—breakfast or lunch, depending on the time of day. It's an hour's run, so there's time to enjoy the food and catch a brief siesta. At other times, when we try to squeeze a meal between or during sets, it's reminiscent of the flurried animation in a silent movie. The long hours, three a.m. to eleven p.m., make the bunk a welcome sanctuary on these runs. Down in the fo'c'sle the noise of the engine is deafening, but stuffing cotton into the ears helps. The rhythmic beat of the engine becomes music, and the vibration is like a gentle massage. The mind is mesmerized while the body relaxes.

After reaching Lopez, Foreigner takes the wheel and follows the contours of the shoreline closely. By hugging the rocks—sometimes the hull is only a few feet off—the skipper takes advantage of the eddies and makes better time when bucking a strong incoming tide. Most of the boats run offshore, which is in our favor because we beat them to Iceberg and get the earlier set.

Iceberg Point is beginning to lose some of its charm, because Tom and I know there's a strong chance that the lead will be called for there. We don't look forward to the back-breaking job of hauling the lead.

Late Friday completes our first week of fishing. With the weekend closure ahead, the boats will return to their home ports and the crews to their homes and families. Foreigner moors at Anacortes and we go on to Everett by car, which saves some of that precious time.

* * *

Early Monday morning we are back at the Griza. The weather has cleared; the ambience of Rosario Strait seems altogether different, and my stomach is once again an uncomplaining part of my anatomy. I am looking forward eagerly to what we all hope will be a good week of fishing. The spirits of the entire crew have improved with the weather. Wearing oilskins for a whole week has a negative effect on one's disposition.

A few boats had made some fair catches off San Juan Island during opening week, which is encouraging. That is where fishermen first meet the salmon as they enter Puget Sound from the North Pacific. We start to catch a few fish on some of our sets, and that always builds morale. Even a few fish suggest promise, which, with the clear, warm weather, makes the hard work and the long hours much easier to take.

The crew of a fishing boat is always hoping for that Big Catch—a plugged hold. That hope is what keeps them returning. They're like the compulsive gambler who goes to Las Vegas year after year in pursuit of that elusive jackpot. Almost every season some lucky boat will be in the right place at the right time and make a big catch—seven or eight thousand salmon in one haul. On those rare occasions, a season's wage is earned in a single day.

The Big Catch is becoming less and less frequent now, more and more a nostalgic memory. The old-timers, like Paul, tell rousing stories of bygone seasons, and almost unbelievable catches.

There's speculation among the seiners that the large fleet of gillnetters in the Sound, especially those congregating at the Salmon Banks, break up the big schools as they come in from the ocean, thus reducing the seiner's chances for the Big Catch. Of course, the gillnetters blame it on the seiners with their huge seines.

Foreigner's "MOLA!" booms often from the bridge, and we make a dozen more hauls a day. Every time I clamber aboard the mother boat from the skiff, Foreigner lashes out with his wounding tongue. Today, it's "What the hell took you so long? You counting the barnacles on the skiff? Get your butt over there and relieve Sam on the purse line!" I have learned to expect this cordial welcome. Seconds later, Foreigner's forced frown turns into a smirk as he pushes the plunger into the water. Pop! "Tra-la-de-do-da . . . bubbles, bubbles, bubbles," he sings joyfully.

Taking the incoming purse line from Sam, I try to coil it as neatly as possible. I glance over at Nels, who is coiling the other purse line, and

detect a faint smile on his face. I think he rather enjoys the skipper's verbal antics. Nel's pile, I see, is coiled perfectly. Mine . . . well, I tell myself, it takes practice.

Quick-witted Bob, forever looking for an opportunity to do some kidding, stands by the winch control. His rotund body is somehow in harmony with his silliness. So are his round face, full jowls and eyes that bug from their sockets like the eyes of a red snapper. He wears a white painter's cap that looks to be several sizes too small. His husky voice seems to come from deep down in his barrel chest.

"Hey, Skipper," he says, "isn't that the *St. Nicholas* brailing over yonder?" (The brailer is a large scoop used to remove fish from the seine when the haul is large. A brailer can hold two or three hundred fish, but it doesn't get much use nowadays.)

"Where?" asks Foreigner with obvious interest, his eyes following the direction of Bob's stare.

Bob roars with belly-shaking hilarity.

"You pig's ass!" Foreigner responds.

Sardine Can (a nickname they've given Paul because they claim he looks like the old salt on the sardine can label) is standing by the winch. He looks at the brailer strapped alongside the cabin and says wistfully, "Our brailer hasn't been used for so long, it's growing moss!"

"I'd sell it for a dollar if anyone offered," Foreigner declares, then adds, "It might be worth more, though, as an antique."

"Excess baggage, that's what it is," Paul says with a note of contempt.

Seagull-Eye Sam, taking advantage of his short break while I pile the purse line, lights up a smoke. "That brailer will be in the water so much it'll grow barnacles on the rim before the season's over," he predicts boldly. He takes a puff on his cigarette, blows out a cloud of smoke, then adds, "In fact, we may have to put on new webbing."

"You ___ ___ windbag!" Foreigner says, then adds wistfully, "I sure hope you're right!"

"Never been wrong yet," Seagull-Eye says.

"Yeah? How about that two-legged jackass

you've got over there in your place? He's making a turd pile out of that purse line!"

"I'm doing my best," I say.

"Hell!" Foreigner barks. "My five-year-old kid could do better!'

I have a powerful yen to use one of Paul's oft-drilled comebacks. With bravado I half-whisper, "*Ti nesna nista—boozdoe.*" (You don't know anything—dumbbell.)

"What?" cries Foreigner.

"I said, that's most likely so."

Nels, the shy one, bewildered by the rough banter going on around him, comes on as the white-robed angel in contrast to Foreigner, the black-robed Lucifer.

Gene, the aloof engineer, emerges from the engine room with the familiar mug and cigarette. He saunters to the after deck, stands by the port davit, stoically watching the proceedings.

"Well, his majesty decided to join the party," Foreigner bellows. "Look at him, boys. Doesn't he look overworked?"

"That coffee grinder of yours takes a lot of attention," Gene asserts.

"Like hell it does! That's the best engine in the fleet. Runs like a Swiss watch." Gene sits on the bulwarks sipping coffee and dragging on his weed, as if he was on a leisurely vacation cruise. A couple of curls hang loosely over his forehead and he wears a cocky look, like the leader of the Dead-End Kids.

Foreigner isn't finished with him. "Look at him, boys! He was down in the engine room looking at a copy of *Sunshine and Health,* and now he needs a rest! He thinks he's on the *Queen Mary!*"

Gene, looking quite unconcerned, takes another drag from his cigarette and another sip from his mug.

"Bubbles, my boys, bubbles!" Foreigner sings as he pops the plunger into the water.

That night we anchor in Aleck Bay near Iceberg Point, where some twenty boats are spending the night. While I'm doing the evening dishes, the rich tones of a trumpet come wafting across the still water and through the galley window. The guy is playing some of the old standards from the 1940s, and he is exceptionally good. For once, scullery duty isn't so boring. As I tap my foot and scrub utensils to the rhythm of the trumpet, Foreigner and Paul converse over a glass of vino. Their subject is stuffing boxes.

The stuffing box is located at the base of the keel, where the propeller shaft penetrates the hull. Its purpose is to keep excessive water from coming in around the shaft. Paul complains to Foreigner that at night he can hear the box dripping. The sound, coming from the rear of the bilge, carries through the engine room and into the fo'c'sle. On most boats, the crew simply learns to live with it. It is not noticeable during the day with the engine running.

Paul's conversation with Foreigner reminds him of another of his many interesting anecdotes. He seems to have an endless number of them, and when he starts to tell one, he captivates an audience. As he talks, he gestures continually with his callused hands, as if punctuating his narrative, and his face, dried and furrowed by many years of exposure to salt and sea, reflects the varying moods of his story.

"A few years ago, on the boat I was fishing, we had a young guy aboard, about nineteen, maybe twenty. First time he'd ever worked on a boat, and he was a real farmer, dripping behind the ears! He came aboard with a suitcase! Can you believe that?" Paul shakes his head and chuckles. "I tell you, this kid was so green, you could have used a lawn-mower on him!

"I felt kinda' sorry for this kid, he seemed so out of place on a seiner. For boots he'd brought a pair that came up to his knees, like the Chinks used to wear in the canneries. When he opened his suitcase you'da thought he was going cruising on some luxury liner! Colognes, powders, I don't know what all! I think he even manicured his fingernails!"

Foreigner, listening, pulls the hair on his left arm. He's being upstaged by Paul, and Foreigner gets nervous when he has to listen.

"The kid had the bunk right above me, wouldn't you know!" Paul's shoulders shake as he chuckles. "Well, one night we were all sitting around after dinner, shooting the bull. We talked about the fo'c'sle and how it was dangerous, because there wasn't any companionway to the deck, like on this boat. You had to go from the galley down through the engine room to get to the damned fo'c'sle. The fellows were saying that if the boat started to sink in the middle of the night, they would have a helluva time getting out of the friggin' fo'c'sle. This green kid was all ears, soaking it up like a sponge does water."

The melodic strains of "Star Dust" waft through the galley window, background music for Paul's story as he continues.

"So comes time to hit the bunks and we all turn in, I go to sleep right away, like I always do on a boat. Along in the middle of the night I hear the damnedest noise! Sounds like all hell broke loose. I can't see a thing, it's that dark, but I hear this kid screaming, 'We're sinking! Let me outta here!' He's scuffling around in the dark, trying to find a way out. 'Help! Help!' he keeps yelling.

"I reach down and feel the floor. It's bone dry, so I know we're not sinking. So I jump out of my bunk and feel around until I get hold of the kid, and shake him and I keep telling him it's okay, we're not sinking. Finally the kid snaps out of it and I lead him back to his bunk. Then, by golly, at breakfast the next morning he denies the whole thing! He says it never happened, and he thinks we're joking with him!"

"Did he last the season?" Gene asks.

"Funny thing. By the end of the season we'd made a man out of him. The crew was on him all the time. He took a lot of crap. However, that's part of the business. Ray will know that before the season's over."

"Raymondo?" Foreigner sneers, "I don't think we'll ever make a man of him!"

Nels smiles apologetically. I wonder how Nels ever got through his first season.

"If you gentlemen are through with the B.S., we got important things to do," Bob announces, and places the shopworn checkerboard on the table. He eliminates four challengers in quick succession, including me. Next weekend I'm picking up a book on checker playing, and it'll be my Bible for the rest of the season.

Later, as the crew is preparing to turn in, I detect a mischievous gleam in Bob's eyes. Now what's he up to?

"Ah, now for a good night's sleep," he says as he snuggles under his blankets. "Pleasant dreams, boys!"

The clutter of boots, oilskins and miscellaneous garb has reduced the already tight confines of the fo'c'sle. There's a stench from the socks airing on makeshift clotheslines. Closing the curtain to my bunk, I block out what's on the other side and nestle in the comparative peace and comfort of my tiny realm.

After a few moments of silence there comes a crackling sound, like the noise of some New Year's Eve novelty. It is intermittent, and disturbing. Finally an irate voice demands to know what's going on.

Someone switches on the light.

"It's coming from Sam's bunk," says another voice.

By now, Sam is stirring and the crackling is continuous. "Some bastard," he barks, "has loaded my mattress!" I can hear him groping and pawing at his mattress, cursing the culprit and declaring evil intent toward the scoundrel who perpetrated this dirty deed. There's a short interval of suspense, and then, "Here's the damned thing!" Sam says with disdain, and tosses a plastic cookie container to the floorboards.

The light is switched off. A snicker, muffled by blankets, comes from Bob's bunk. Then all is silent in the fo'c'sle.

Crewman throws "figure eight" clear as seine is laid out. Figure eights are metal links in the purse line. Note purse line through purse ring.

Nels makes sure corkline is clear as seine is laid out.

Tom watches for entanglements as lead net pays out over stern of skiff.

Tom holds coil of line – ready to throw – as Emancipator approaches. Note how skiff acts as a link between lead net and seine.

Gene, subbing for Raymondo on this set, tosses throw line to receiver on mother boat.

Crew pile seine coming down from power block. Seine must be piled neatly so it doesn't tangle during layout.

Paul and Sam "pursing-up" as lines come off winch.

A neat coil of purse line is necessary to keep it from entangling when seine is laid out.

View from top of deckhouse (note photographer's boot in foreground.) Foreigner "plunges" as purse lines emerge from water, pass through davits on way to winch.

During a "purse-up" purse lines come off winch and Sam and Nels coil them neatly on deck.

Paul, Bob, Sam and Nels working purse lines and breast lines through winch.

The purse rings are lowered as Paul, Nels, Sam, Gene, Foreigner and Bob guide them to the deck. At this stage the salmon are entrapped within the seine.

The power-block, back-saver to the fishermen, pulls seine from water as crew pile.

Crew begin piling seine coming down from power block.

With the aid of the power block, crew piles last few fathoms of seine.

5

THE STRIKE

DURING THE THIRD WEEK OF FISHING, TALK
of a strike begins to circulate around the fleet.
The canneries are paying twenty-eight cents
a pound for sockeyes, the same price they paid
during the previous two years, yet the price of
canned sockeye has risen substantially. The fishermen feel they're entitled to a share of the additional profit.

The fleet ties up at Anacortes to do battle
with the canneries.

The union, Fishermen's Division
of the International Longshoremen's and
Warehousemen's Union, proves to be weak in
representing the fishermen. At the start of the
season, a union official had come down to the
docks asking for the twenty-dollar membership
dues. Maybe a quarter of the fleet joined. The
rest told the union representative to get lost.
To pay dues to a union that did nothing for the
fishermen was money down the drain; about as
useless as betting on the Pittsburgh Pirates to win
the National League pennant (something they
hadn't done since the last ice-skater left Lake
Okeechobee).

Lacking a strong union, the fishermen
decide to get together and do their own bargaining
with the canneries. They rent a hall and hold a
meeting to agree on what price to demand. The
fishermen, more than a thousand in number,
agree to ask for thirty-five cents a pound for
sockeye salmon. The canneries counter with an
offer of thirty-two cents. What follows is a week
of dickering.

With the peak of the season nearing, some
of the fishermen get itchy. They want to salvage
some kind of season, so during the negotiations,
about twenty boats break the picket line and go
out fishing. The rest of the fishermen are roaring
mad. There are cries of "Shoot the bastards!"
and "Blackball the scabs!" and "Hang 'em all!"

With the scabs weakening their bargaining
power against the canneries, the fishermen call
for another meeting to decide how to punish the
scabs. Some drastic measures are proposed, but
finally it's decided that violence is not the answer.
Someone suggests renting a small plane and
taking aerial pictures of all the boats fishing during
the strike. The idea is that, with photographic
evidence, the scabs can be blackballed from the
union and employers can be discouraged from
hiring any of the renegades.

The chairman asks for a volunteer with
experience in aerial photography. I raise my
hand and tell the group that, having been an
aerial photographer in the Navy, I could do the
shooting. As no one else volunteers, it is agreed
unanimously to send me on "Mission Scab
Reconnaissance."

It is only three years since I left the Navy,
where my job entailed aerial photography and
mapping, so I have confidence in my ability to take
the pictures. The problem is that the only camera
I have with me is an antique four-by-five Conley,
well past its glory days and a misfit for the job. I'd
brought it along because I'm not concerned for
its welfare under seine-boat conditions. My good
camera, a German Rollieflex, is safely at home.

Early next morning the chosen pilot, a
spokesman for the fishermen, and I hold a brief

Aerial view of seine boat in a set at Eagle Pt. The skiff is keeping her clear of the seine.

meeting to discuss procedure. We are to fly over the various fishing areas, and when we spot a boat with its seine in the water, circle at low altitude around the boat so I can photograph it in operation.

Shortly after eight a.m. the pilot and I board a small Cessna and lift off the water of Guemes Channel, heading for the salmon banks off the southern shore of San Juan Island. I am clutching my relic four-by-five, designed for portrait and landscape but not aerial photography. However, I'm not expected to bring back a Rembrandt, just a recognizable photographic record of the scab boats in action.

It's a brilliant day. Never having flown over the San Juan Islands, I am excited. The pilot banks the plane to port and we head toward Rosario Strait. There we scan the water for scab boats, but there are none in sight. We head for Deception Pass to check out the West Beach and the Griza, my skipper's favorite spot. No boats in sight at those locations either, so we turn west again and head for Iceberg Point.

As we fly across the ten miles of open water, the pilot points out the window and says, "Look there!"

A large pod of killer whales, I'd guess seventy-five to a hundred, is traveling east toward Deception Pass. Their large dorsal fins break the smooth surface of the water. All fishermen know that the presence of killer whales means the presence of salmon in abundance. I shudder at the thought that schools of sockeye, possibly millions of individuals, are swimming down there, and the whales are stuffing themselves, while the boats are tied up in Anacortes.

We reach Iceberg and still there are no boats in sight. I'm beginning to think we're on a wild goose chase. A few minutes later we fly over Mackaye Harbor and see a few seiners, but they're at anchor. We fly on toward Eagle Point and the Salmon Banks. As we near Eagle Point, the pilot motions with his chin toward the windshield. Straight ahead I see seine boats, six of them, and as we get closer we can see that each has a seine in the water and in some stage of a haul. We circle one boat after another, as low as we can safely fly. I wait until we are in position to see the name on the bow, then snap the shutter. We're so close we can see the crew looking up at us as if they expect us to open fire on them.

I take a couple pictures of each boat, but I must conserve film. I have only two more packets of twelve exposures each, and four-by-five film isn't something you pick up at the nearest drug store.

None of these boats is at the end of the set, so we can't tell whether they are catching any fish.

We continue to Mitchell Bay and, as we near it, see more seiners. When we get closer, I count eight boats with their seines in the water. The pilot banks to starb'rd to allow me good shots at the boats. While I snap the shutter, I wonder whether I am getting good pictures with this relic.

One of the boats is brailing. That means he's making a good haul. No wonder; those scabs have the grounds to themselves, with ninety-five percent of the fleet tied up in port. If the striking fishermen hear about this, they're likely to forget about the strike and rush to the grounds.

After we photograph all eight boats, we head up Haro Strait toward Point Roberts to check out the area around Boundary Bay. Flying over Henry and Stuart Islands, we see no more boats. The weather is perfect and our altitude gives us a spectacular view of the San Juan Islands. They look like a brown and green flotilla anchored in a sea of emerald. As we head toward Point Roberts, a large freighter steams down Haro Strait, most likely bound for Seattle from Alaska.

No boats are fishing at either Point Roberts or Boundary Bay. It looks as if the Point Roberts fleet is being true to the cause. We turn south and fly over Cherry Point and Lummi Island before heading back down Rosario Strait. We touch down at Anacortes shortly before noon, having made a complete circle of the major fishing areas in Puget Sound. If my ancient Conley delivers, we now have a permanent record of who's scabbing.

At the meeting next day, the spokesman informs the striking fishermen that "scab reconnaissance" found fourteen boats fishing, but was unsure of their catches. The spokesman felt, and we agreed, that it was better for the fishermen to stay in port and continue bargaining with the canneries.

Negotiations continue for the rest of the week, and by late Saturday, the fishermen agree to accept the canneries' offer of thirty-two cents a pound. On Sunday morning the fleet heads for the fishing grounds, anxious to make up for lost time.

Sam and skipper look for jumpers on Rosario Strait.

6

THE LONG, HOT SUMMER

WITH THE TWO-WEEK-LONG STRIKE settled, the fishermen are eager to get back to work. They are concerned that they may have missed the best runs of the season while on strike. According to rumors from the north, the Canadian fishermen had some good catches while the Americans where on strike.

The International Sockeye Commission, between the United States and Canada, was established to allocate the sockeye harvest fairly between the two countries. Its primary job is to see that each country gets fifty percent of the harvestable fish. If either country surges ahead, the Commission will close down its fishery while the other country catches up. Through the years, the Commission has managed an even distribution of this valuable resource. Now that the Canadian fishermen have built up a big lead, the cry of the American fleet is, "Catch up with the Canadians!" Word is spreading that we will fish continually until we catch up with our neighbors to the north.

At Anacortes we load extra groceries and extra clothes, as no one knows what to expect in the days ahead. The weather has turned hot and humid, with high temperatures near ninety degrees, and more heat in the forecast. No one cares, however; we're anxious to get back to making a living.

The crew seems to have added energy during the long rest. Paul is bouncing around the deck like a prizefighter in training, shadow-boxing an invisible foe. Bob is singing in the galley, and no doubt dreaming up his next practical joke. Foreigner, at the wheel, chews more vigorously on his cigar stub, while the wheels of decision spin in his mind. Sam, sitting next to Foreigner, sweeps his seagull eyes across the waters. Gene has a cockier-than-usual look. The hot weather doesn't reduce his caffeine consumption. His faithful companion hangs from his hooked finger. Nels, more relaxed now around the "crazy Croats," is contributing an occasional line. Tom, as if cleansed by two whole weeks of freedom from Foreigner's put-downs, has an added sparkle. I, too, have regained some self-respect, some stature as a human being—I wonder how long it will last.

We fish the Griza the first day, catch fifty to a hundred per set, and total around six hundred for the day. Late in the afternoon, Foreigner calls his pal, Frank, skipper of the *Gladiator*. Frank is considered a kingpin in the Lime Kiln area, while Foreigner has a reputation as a highliner at the Griza. When either area gets hot, it's time for radio contact.

The radio is a useful device for crafty fishermen who want to let their buddies in on some good fishing. A straightforward broadcast of such a message would bring the entire fleet racing to the hot spot, but they've developed their own coy ways of communicating. Foreigner and Frank, both avid pigskin fans, use the Notre Dame football team as their private code. Certain key words in their apparently casual talk convey their messages.

Early next morning, the *Gladiator* has reached the Griza, joining the eight or so regulars of the Griza fleet. Although Foreigner has invited his buddy to come and share the good fishing, they now become fierce competitors. Just another of the enigmas of fishing.

While Foreigner is blinking his eyes, Frank initiates a set off Northwest Rock. As soon as his seine is in the water, the sockeye begin jumping. Foreigner, irked because Frank has beaten him to the punch, sets behind, hoping to catch the overflow from the *Gladiator's* seine. As soon as we've set, a couple of jumpers show in our seine. That always gets the adrenaline flowing; a jumper or two usually indicates a school of fish.

The show produces much excitement at the towhead. Spreading with blazing speed, it afflicts every boat at the Griza, and the frenzy is on. Whereas our earlier sets at the Griza were ho-hum affairs, our expectations mount. Tom looks eager and earnest. I feel a surge of excitement. Now we're seeing more and more jumpers between our skiff and the mother boat. We've been towing only a short while when Foreigner gives Tom the signal to close. The skiff, though under full throttle, labors slowly toward the mother boat.

As soon as we're alongside, I leap aboard. The crew is working feverishly on the deck. By now, we've become a team, and things are going smoothly. We purse, haul the rings, and begin to pick up. While we're piling the seine on the stern, we see the *Gladiator* using her brailer a short distance away. Bob, who never misses a chance to introduce some satire into the situation, says, "Frank'll hafta put new webbing on his brailer after this set. He's working the hell out of it!"

Foreigner, feeling that the *Gladiator's* set should have been his, is not amused. "Whatever we get will be his leftovers," he says ruefully.

When we get to the end of the seine, Foreigner orders me into the skiff, "Quick, like a bunny!" I crawl over the bulwarks and jump into the skiff. Tom is busy tying a line around the cork line of the seine.

"Raymondo! Tie those corks!" Foreigner screams. "Pull those corks into the skiff! Push away! Push away!"

Bewildered, I freeze with a stupid look on my face. Tom rushes over and performs the duties.

"You're as useless as a damned statue!" Foreigner yells. "Dry up the bundt!"

Now I'm totally confused. No one has instructed me in the fine art of brailing. Hadn't the crew agreed, not so many hours ago, that the brailer is obsolete? I look up. Three or four feet above me I see the blurred images of six men bending over the rail. Their mouths, moving simultaneously, bark unfamiliar orders at me.

"Pull that web! Over there, *boozdoe!*"

"Push the skiff away! QUICK!"

"Dry up the web! Hurry! Hurry!"

I feel like yelling, "One at a time, please!" However, I realize there's no use trying to change the established ritual. I scramble around, trying the best I can to obey their ambiguous commands. I notice Tom pulling web into the skiff, so I start clawing at the web like a desperate dog digging for a bone.

"Pull hard and it'll come easy!" bellows Foreigner, for the umpteenth time.

After minutes of what seems like mass hysteria, Tom and I get the bundt dried up. The fish, now massed in the confines of the bundt, are splashing wildly, trying to escape. Salt water is splashing as if from an overhead fountain.

The crew readies the brailer. It comes whirling down from the boom overhead—a metal hoop about four feet in diameter attached to a big black net bag with a chain-controlled opening at its end. The brailer is pushed forcefully into the bundt to scoop up the frantic fish. Someone on deck holds tension on the chain while the brailer is lifted and swung over the hold, where the net is emptied.

As the brailer drops into the bundt, the crew erupts in a chorus of commands:

"Pull the web!"

"Dry 'er up! Dry it! Dry it!"

"Over there! That web! Pull it! Pull it!"

"Roll 'em in! Roll 'em in!"

It takes three scoops of the brailer to empty the bundt. After the last scoop, Foreigner bellows, "You guys brail like a bunch of farmers! A couple hundred fish, and it takes three scoops! If we ever get a few thousand, it'll take you jerks the rest of the season to brail 'em!"

Our catch is about four hundred fish.

Gladiator has taken four thousand—thanks to the Fighting Irish.

Some skippers travel from one location to another in pursuit of the sockeye. Foreigner concentrates on the Griza and Iceberg. Today we run from the Griza to Iceberg, stopping in Rosario Strait to look for jumpers. As the boat drifts with the current, we all strain our eyes looking across the glaring water in search of a jumper. If one is sighted, Foreigner will set. If not, we can relax for a few minutes.

While I wait, I rest my weary head on the bow of the skiff and prop my legs on the engine housing. The rest of me fits nicely on the small deck in the bow. The gentle motion of the sea lulls me toward sleep; after all, they don't need me to watch for jumpers, Seagull-Eye Sam is on the bridge. Having him there is as good as having an eagle perched on a tall spar. Besides, the seine pile hides me from Foreigner's view, so it should be safe to doze for a brief interlude.

No sooner has my subconscious taken over than an ear-splitting roar jerks me to my feet. There, kneeling on the stern of the mother boat, is Bob holding a three-foot-long foghorn. A blast from that thing could rouse a dead gull. "The skipper said to look for jumpers," Bob tells me. I tell him he can use his foghorn for a suppository. He guffaws loudly as he walks away, his flabby sides shaking like molded gelatin.

We move on to Iceberg. We make a set close to the beach without much success, so Foreigner moves out a little way from shore to look around. Sam, standing on the bridge beside Foreigner, nods and whispers to him. He has spotted a jumper. It's risky for a crewman to yell or point to indicate the sighting of a jumper. If nearby boats catch the signal, they might beat you to the set.

Quickly Foreigner maneuvers the boat into position for a set. Another boat has sighted the jumper and is positioning for a set. It's going to be a race.

"Mola!" Foreigner yells. The skiff leaves the stern, and Tom swings it half-circle within a second. The prop churns the water as Tom throttles the skiff to full speed. The *Susan* passes, at full speed, within twenty-feet of our bow. There's a clatter as the *Susan's* pelican hook releases her skiff, and in seconds her seine comes reeling off her stern. There's no question about what's happening; we are getting what seiners call a "royal corking."

Foreigner brings the *Emancipator* to a halt within close range of the *Susan*. Sam stands up on the bench of the bridge, bends forward with his back towards her, drops his trousers, and exposes his bare bottom to the passing skipper. That is his way of saying, "Thanks a million!"

In the skiff, Tom stops the towing and releases the seine. We speed back to the mother boat, tie up alongside, and rush to the stern.

Now comes the fun. We have to pick up the seine by hand—without the aid of the power block. The entire crew pulls at the heavy seine. We've laid out about sixty fathoms and now, heavy and dripping with saltwater, it has to be pulled back aboard. It's back-breaking work and is accompanied by some uncomplimentary remarks about the *Susan's* skipper. He will be cursed for the rest of the season and into the next.

Being corked is not a pleasant experience, but it happens many times during the season. When "fish fever" afflicts some skippers, they tend to forget their manners. An automobile driver can sympathize with the seiner when he experiences a landlubber version of corking. Did you ever pull up at a parallel parking space, intending to back in, only to have some wise guy barge head-first into the stall? Getting corked is an upsetting experience. We'll be bitter for awhile, but too busy to brood.

For the next several days we divide our fishing time between the Griza and Iceberg, and average four to five hundred fish a day. A rumor circulating among the boats has it that some are making good catches at the Salmon Banks.

Suddenly the radio comes alive. "Calling *Emancipator*. This is *Gladiator*. Come in, please." Foreigner answers the call, and it isn't long before the two skippers bring up Notre Dame. Immediately after the over-and-out, Foreigner heads us toward Eagle Point and the Salmon

Banks. This is new territory for us. We're leaving the security of our familiar nest. I've heard fishermen talk about Eagle Point, Mitchell Bay, Lime Kiln and Open Bay, and of course, I saw them from the air on Mission Scab Reconnaissance; but that's quite different from experiencing them at sea level. These places are connected with tales of fierce competition among the boats. They're where the big boys hang out, the top fishermen, the boats with fleet-wide reputations—*Sea Master, Barbara S, Dreamland, Star of Heaven, Freeland* and the rest of the elite.

Fishermen claim that Eagle Point is where the salmon, coming in from the ocean, divide according to the routes they take to reach the mouth of the Fraser River in British Columbia. The fish that take the east course head toward Iceberg and up through Rosario Strait. They pass Lummi Island, Cherry Point and Boundary Bay. At Point Roberts, they join their conspecifics which have taken the westerly course past Mitchell Bay, Henry Island and Stuart Island, and all proceed up Georgia Strait.

When we arrive at Eagle Point, we find fifty or sixty boats milling around or in sets. Foreigner looks for a place to drop the seine, but the waters are already congested. We run offshore a little way, where the boats thin out, and look for jumpers. After a few minutes, Foreigner gets impatient and decides on a blind set (setting without having seen a jumper). We are rewarded with three hundred sockeye.

Boats close to the beach are brailing. We move closer to shore and get a good set off Eagle Point. It proves to be our best so far. We pick up a thousand or more. Most sets here are on the blind, as the competition is so fierce there isn't time to look for signs.

The lead net isn't used here, so already I like the place.

That evening, we run to the lee of Cattle Point to meet the cannery tender and deliver our fish. The seiner doesn't have to handle ice. As fast as the fish come aboard, they go into the hold, which isn't much warmer than the surrounding sea. Each evening, the cannery tender comes to the grounds, picks up the day's catch, and takes it to the cannery. Griffin Bay is full of activity, as fifty or more boats are unloading or waiting to unload. We wait more than an hour before the Whitney-Fidalgo tender is free to take us.

Tom, Gene, Sam and I "volunteer" for hatch duty. Armed with pickaroons, like soldiers of antiquity, we enter the smelly, slimy confines of the hold. The large brailer from the tender's boom is lowered into the hold. The four of us position ourselves around the brailer and pitch fish into it as fast as we can. From the deck above, Foreigner yells down at us, "Okay, you knuckleheads, let's not take all night. Other boats are waiting."

"Easy for you," Gene responds impassively. "Come on down and show us how it's done."

"Hell, I can pitch faster than the four of you combined!" snaps Foreigner.

"Yeah, if his hands could move as fast as his mouth!" Tom mutters, out of Foreigner's hearing.

Each of us pitches fifty fish. The brailer is lifted, weighed, emptied into the tender, then lowered back into the hold for a refill. We unload a total of twenty-five hundred fish. By quick calculation, if each fish is worth two dollars, then twenty-five hundred fish are worth $5,000; and if each crewmember gets eight percent of the catch, then the share per man equals $400. Not bad for a day's work.

We anchor here in Griffin Bay, which, for eleven months of the year, is isolated and quiet. Quiet? Not now! Even at this late hour it is resounding with noise: fishermen's voices, boats unloading, diesels running, winches humming, machinery clattering, chains clanking through bow saddles, and anchors splashing. Tonight, with the lights of so many boats and tenders, it looks like a small city.

It's eleven o'clock when we finally get around to dinner. It's been a long day. We have toiled since three-thirty this morning , but we're feeling upbeat. When the fishing is good, the fisherman doesn't notice fatigue until he flops onto his bunk. Even then, it's a pleasurable tiredness, knowing the hard labor has brought reward.

After polishing off one of Bob's superb meals (T-bone steak, potatoes and salad), the crew sits idly savoring the silence that follows a good meal—the final applause. Foreigner lights up a cigar—it seems a ritual by now—and puffs with renewed confidence and pride. We sip our wine and feel at ease.

Outside, a full moon beams down on the scene, as if an omen. Its shaft of light seems to be focused here and nowhere else.

Next morning, we return to Eagle Point. Word has spread through the fleet that the fishing is good here, so now there's a large concentration of hopeful seiners. We make three sets in the morning, with far less success than we had enjoyed yesterday. The fish are here, but with so much gear in the water, the individual shares are smaller.

In the afternoon, we run over to Iceberg and make a set. When we start to pick up the seine, we are bombarded with red jellyfish.

These weird gelatinous creatures may have some beneficial part to play in the overall scheme of marine ecology, but no fisherman who has encountered them would lament their extinction. The largest specimens are four feet or more in diameter. Their tentacles, up to six feet long, are studded with cells that exude a stinging fluid. To human skin it causes inflammation and an intense burning sensation that lasts for hours. Rubbing the affected area increases the discomfort. If a man has the misfortune to get a splash of this red venom in the eye, he can expect hours of near blindness and excruciating pain.

At the first sight of this marine menace, Foreigner orders Bob to stop the power block and we all put on special gear to protect ourselves. Besides the familiar oilskins, we put on rubber gloves, arm shields, eye protectors and anything else that might shield a part of our person. Gene, having the most vulnerable position—piling the leads—wears a welder's mask to shield his John Garfield looks. Even so, some of the irritating fluid manages to find its way to the skin. The hot weather we're experiencing stimulates the sweat glands, which open the pores to the invading fluid. When the jellyfish come in overwhelming numbers, the crew has to expect some hours of misery.

The seine carries the jellyfish up through the power block, where they are shredded and mixed with saltwater and then come raining down on the crew as a red slush. Nevertheless, the seine must be brought aboard. After the set, we wash down the deck to remove all the bits and pieces. Some of the larger jellyfish, having been removed from the seine before it went through the power block, are intact. Trying to pick up one of those and throw it overboard is like trying to cradle a cow's entrails.

It's necessary to wash all your personal gear thoroughly, as the stinging power of the venom remains for several hours. Neglecting to wash the hands can result in discomfort later, especially if one needs to relieve himself soon after coping with a jellyfish-laden haul.

The seine, piled on the stern, looks like a mass of pulp left over from a wine-making operation. Foreigner decides to run over to Rosario Strait and make a set to clean the seine. Minutes after we reach the strait, Seagull Eye spots a jumper, so Foreigner circles the seine around the frolicking fish. No sooner have we laid out, than a rip tide races towards the seine with threatening force. A rip tide is two opposing currents moving in opposite directions. When it's strong enough, it can cause considerable damage to a seine—tear it to ribbons or swallow it completely. The force is awesome, and much feared.

Foreigner, seeing the approaching danger, orders Tom to close immediately. The rip tide charges the boat and seine with amazing speed. Before we can close, the tide starts working the seine as if the two opposing forces are waging a tug-of-war for possession of it. The seine flattens out within seconds. The corks, instead of forming a large circle, are forced together and slap at one another the entire length of the net. The seine is like a deflated, shriveled balloon. We are in a state of emergency.

Foreigner orders Tom to tow one end of the seine, trying to straighten out the bunched-up mess. Aboard the mother boat, the crew starts to pick up the other end of the seine through the power block. It's hard going. The seine, thanks to the rip tide, resists stubbornly. At short intervals Foreigner stops the power block while the crew works furiously to clear the web from the corks, which have clustered and entangled the web. It's stop! Untangle. Apply power. Stop! Untangle! This goes on for two hours, but finally we get the seine aboard.

With evening approaching, Foreigner figures we have time for one more haul. We look around Rosario, and Seagull Eye locates another jumper. The seine reels off the stern and away we go, feeling that Murphy's Law has run its course. Wrong!

As we start to pick, gilled dogfish begin to come up in the seine. This particular creature is right up there with the red jellyfish on the fisherman's least-wanted list. It is one of the smallest sharks, growing up to five feet long. In smell its flesh is strongly reminiscent of urine, but its liver is one of the richest known sources of Vitamin A. So is the soupfin shark's liver; however, the soupfin population is scant, whereas the dogfish is numerous and ubiquitous in the North Pacific and North Atlantic. During World War II, the dogfish fishery was highly profitable, and the population thinned out. Then came synthetic Vitamin A, which was cheaper, and again the dogfish became worthless and ubiquitous.

Now, here they are, coming up with our seine, as thick as grapes on a vine. Bob stops the power block every few seconds and we all pick dogfish off the seine. We grab the leathery creatures, being careful not to get punctured by the wicked spine in front of each of the two dorsal fins (they can lacerate and infect the hand, and a wounded hand is not what the fisherman needs). We then pull the thing free of the web, bash its head against the deck, and throw it overboard. This series of maneuvers is performed to a chorus of profanity. It has been a hard but unproductive day, and the crew is taking it out on the dogfish.

"We shoulda stayed at anchor this morning," Sam laments as he sends another dogfish flying.

"That's for sure," Foreigner agrees.

"If this was 1942, we'd be rich!" says Paul, the eternal optimist.

"Yeah, and if the queen had a mustache she'd be king!" Gene adds.

It's totally dark by the time we pick the last dogfish from the seine. We must have picked a thousand of them. We head for the anchorage with our tails between our legs. Today's performance has cut yesterday's payday in half. At dinner, Paul summarizes the fisherman's chances.

"You know, Raymondo," he says, looking across the table at me, "you're going to find that this is a crazy business. One day it's chicken, next day it's feathers."

"Hell, we didn't even get the feathers," Gene reminds him. "All we got was the s___!"

"Rip tide, jellyfish, dogfish! What else could happen?" Foreigner says. "I felt like it was fourth and twenty on our own two-yard line.

"And you fumbled!" Gene taunts him.

Foreigner whips his hat across Gene's curly head, then states with a gust, "Fumbled, hell! I gambled and lost. You have to gamble in this business. It's the only way to make it. Sometimes you win, sometimes you lose. Today we lost."

"We'll hafta bench Sam," says Bob, as he places food on the table. "His seagull eyes are failing."

"That *was* a salmon," Sam insists. "It jumped twice."

"And each jump meant five hundred dogfish below," Bob retorts.

"Well, I'm glad he didn't jump four or five times!" says Paul. "We'd still be out there pickin' dogfish!"

Bob again: "Maybe we can find a market for dogfish and forget about salmon."

"Maybe we can find a market for B.S.," Foreigner says. "The way it flows from your mouth, we could all get rich!"

Tom, from his corner: "I knew I shoulda left my boots on!"

Gene, from his stool: "Too deep for boots, Tom. You need a body sheath."

After a day of disasters, fishermen often

resort to raillery to disguise their disappointment.

The fo'c'sle is like a sauna. The heat from the engine, combined with the hot weather, makes it almost intolerable. This unexpected, long interval of clear, hot weather in the Puget Sound area suggests El Niño; the warm current that, on occasion, moves northward from the tropics and brings along with it some exotic marine species. Each day dawns with the promise of another perfect day. Each sunset assures us that tomorrow will be the same as today. Such weather is a treat to Northwesterners, though our tongues tend to hang out when the mercury reaches into the high eighties and even the nineties. The crew, after long hours of exposure to the sun day after day, looks like a band of Kanakas on an Ahi boat off the Kona Coast!

After two weeks of fishing without a break, Foreigner decides to run in to Anacortes to refuel, re-provision, and let the crew take much needed showers. Our stay is short and we return to the Griza. The word around the fleet is that the Canadians are still substantially ahead of us, so it seems we're in for another long stretch of fishing.

Fishing the Griza proves only modestly rewarding. We make some good catches at first, but more boats begin fishing Deception Island and West Beach. Those two locations, a short distance from the Griza, are where fish bound for the Griza can be intercepted. Inevitably, production drops at the Griza.

Meanwhile there's a rumor circulating through the fleet that a huge run of sockeyes is about to enter the straits. Rumors race continually among the boats. They're part of the game. Although most rumors can be taken with a grain of salt, they add excitement. After all, maybe this one is true! This latest rumor has it that a large, dark mass—two miles wide and ten miles long—has been sighted off the west coast of Vancouver Island. This huge school, many millions of salmon, should enter the Strait of Juan de Fuca and be at the Salmon Banks in a day or two.

Another clue, and this is fact, not rumor, is that literally hundreds of killer whales are lurking in Puget Sound, waiting for the salmon.

All this, including the low productivity at the Griza, lights a fire under Foreigner's *gazitsa*. We head west toward the Salmon Banks. As we cross Rosario Strait, we pass a very large pod of killer whales. Their dorsal fins, some six feet or more tall, are mesmerizing to the watcher as they move gracefully up and down. Paul declares this is the largest concentration of killer whales he has ever seen in his long career of fishing—probably a hundred or more in the pod.

After the two-hour run from the Griza, we are milling around the Salmon Banks. We are about to compete with the big boys, the elite of the fleet—boats with reputations. The presence of these boats stimulates more excitement, as we know there must be fish wherever these boats congregate. Boats of lesser reputation have come, too. I'd guess there are around two hundred seine boats between Cattle Point and Open Bay.

We make three sets by Eagle Point and pick up seven to eight hundred fish. There's a good showing, and many of the boats are using their brailers.

With all this competition, the action is lively. If a skipper stops to scratch his nose, he may lose a set. What would be called corking in another area is standard practice here. Nonetheless, Foreigner stays with the big boys and battles them like the fighting Irish of Notre Dame.

The boats are so heavily congested around Eagle Point that Tom sometimes has to maneuver around another seine or two to reach the mother boat and close the seine. It isn't unusual, here and there, to bump guards with another boat. We get dirty looks from flying bridges, and profanity flows from the decks.

When Foreigner figures the tide is right, we break from the pack and head west toward Mitchell Bay. As we pass the Lime Kiln Lighthouse, Foreigner salutes the *Gladiator*. Frank is in a set at his favorite spot. The many bow waves behind us indicate that a substantial part of the fleet is pursuing the same plan Foreigner has is mind.

Whenever we travel from one fishing ground to another, Tom and I take the opportunity to get

Starting a set – for naught; boat in background is giving us a royal corking.

out of the skiff. Usually we climb to the flying bridge to watch the scenery go by. Foreigner's unpredictable behavior is sometimes entertaining. Today he is singing names of boats as they appear on the horizon, heading our way. He has an uncanny ability to recognize boats at such a distance that, to Tom and me, they look like specks on the horizon.

Joyfully, he sings. "*Vigilant*, oh *Vigilant*, turn thy bow around. *Fort Bragg*, go back to California! Beaver, beaver, *Oregon City*, you're in Husky territory. Go west, *Western Maid*, go west!"

Each boat has her individuality, a uniqueness that distinguishes her from every other boat. The *Sea Master*, one of the fastest boats in the fleet, has a flared bow that pushes a large, white, ominous bow wave. She can be distinguished at a great distance. She demands respect, and she gets it. One of her major concerns, however, is shaking

parasitic boats. The *Dreamland*, with her high bow and low pilothouse, appears to be lurking among the other boats like a sly fox. Somehow she emanates an air of mystery.

If the fishermen were asked to pick the best skipper of the fleet, they'd almost certainly select Paul Serka, skipper of the *Sea Master*, and Paul Martinis, skipper of the *Dreamland*. Both have fished for more than forty years, and their records justify the respect accorded them.

Paul and Seagull Eye have joined us on the flying bridge to look for jumpers. With five sets of eyes topside, we should be able to spot any splashes. We pass what is known in fishing circles as the Big Rock, on the eastern end of Andrews Bay. Four boats are milling around the rock in a daily ritual that the fleet has come to expect. Paul tells me about it.

"Well, you see, the sockeyes school up in

Seine boats anchored at Griffin Bay, San Juan Island. L to R: St. Nicholas, Westwind, Vigilant, Golden Gate, Sierra Seas, Gladiator, Emancipator, Katherine M, Kansas, Hollywood, Pt. Defiance, Lemes.

that bay and come out when the tide changes. Not a minute earlier, and not a minute later, right on the split second. There's only space for one set, so these guys are playing a chess game. Always the same four boats, and they won't let anyone else in.

"The tide has to be exactly right when the boat sets, or its seine will get carried onto a snag. Just seconds make the difference between a good set and disaster. It's all in the timing and positioning, so they usually start half an hour before the tide changes. They mill around casually at first, but the tension builds up. All four skippers keep their eyes on the kelp near the rock. That's the clue. The exact instant the kelp starts to swing, that's when the tide is changing, and whichever boat is in the right position is the lucky one. The skipper yells, 'Mola!' and out goes the seine.

"But if he leaves the tiniest splinter of daylight, he may get corked. It's a crazy game, but the payoff is worth it. They get some mighty big sets there."

This is out of our league, so we pass the chess game and go on to Little Rock, about a mile west of Big Rock. The configuration here is more to Foreigner's liking and the competition isn't so fierce.

As we come abreast of the rock, Seagull Eye whispers something to Foreigner. Without warning, Foreigner yells, "Get into the skiff, quick!" Tom and I slide down the ladder and race for the stern. Foreigner shouts, "Mola!" from the bridge just as Tom leaps into the skiff.

The Lime Kiln lighthouse on the southern shore of San Juan Island. The seiner Gladiator's favorite hangout.

The pelican hook clanks and the bow of the skiff drops from the stern of the mother boat. There's space between the two as I jump for the skiff. I land on the small bow deck and scramble to keep from falling overboard. Tom swings the skiff half-circle and the seine comes reeling off the mother boat. Foreigner has the *Emancipator* racing full speed, trying to encircle the school of sockeye. As the last fathom of seine drops into the water, we see the competition bearing down on us. It seems a good share of the fleet is steaming into the bay like a massive herd of buffalo.

As Tom and I tow the end of the seine we can see finners moving into it. This is my first experience with finners, and it's like a shot of adrenaline. To look across the water and see hundreds of salmon fins breaking the smooth surface—well, it's enough to supercharge the most phlegmatic fisherman.

By now, other boats have seen the show and are setting expectantly near us.

As soon as the finners have passed between the mother boat and the skiff, Foreigner orders us to close the seine. Salmon will enter a seine and swim until they encounter the fence-like obstruction. Then, sensing danger, they either dive or swim out. This is by far the best showing we've had all season, and Foreigner doesn't want to lose any by towing too long.

As we purse the seine, the water inside the circle of corks is boiling with finners and jumpers. To call this exciting is an understatement.

After we've picked up, Tom pulls the skiff alongside. Tom and I are now working more efficiently together, and the yelling from the deck has quieted enough that we can understand the instructions. The crew starts to brail, and brail, and brail—about thirty times! That means about six thousand sockeye in one haul, the best of the season by far. I make a quick calculation and come up with nine hundred dollars for each man on the crew. A good day's pay by any standards.

Here's how the share principle works: The skipper and each member of the crew gets one share. The boat and seine get four shares. That makes twelve shares, so each man on the crew receives one-twelfth of the total take. However, from his share he pays one-eighth of the cost of fuel and food.

That night we anchor near Mosquito Pass, between San Juan and Henry Islands, in a quiet little bay with barely enough room for half a dozen boats. A stone house on the beach is the only indication of development in sight. The owners of that house have their own little paradise in this isolated spot. That night the crew sleeps as soundly as the drift logs lying on the beach, just a few fathoms from our hull.

Before daybreak, we are up for our early morning mug-up. The small bay is even more dazzling in this hour before dawn. The swath of a full August moon reflects across the tranquil water. It's enough to capture a man's soul. Even the most skillful artist would find it hard to do this scene justice.

The mug-up is a good way to start the fisherman's day—a few quiet moments before the hectic pace begins, a time to reflect upon yesterday's success and look hopefully, expectantly, to today. In the quiet atmosphere of this Shangri La, this morning seems special.

Suddenly the spell is shattered as Foreigner comes bursting into the galley like a firecracker in a monastery. "Okay, you misfits, let's get this show on the road! You think you're on vacation? Think you can sit around and listen to the birds chirping?"

"Relax," Gene says, caressing the coffee mug in his hand.

"Relax, my butt! We have all winter to relax. Now's the time to suffer! Suffer, my boys! Suffer!"

Gene, unruffled, sips his coffee. "Easy for you, skipper. All you have to do come winter is sit around and count your money."

"Oh, sure!" Foreigner barks. "If I listened to you, we'd be sittin' around drinking coffee all day and there wouldn't be any money to count."

Bob hands Foreigner a steaming mug. "Here, try this melted tar," he says. "It'll get your spark plugs firing."

"My spark plugs are already firing," Foreigner retorts, then he looks over at me. "It'll take more than coffee to get Raymondo moving. He needs a firecracker under his ass." (Please! Don't give Bob that idea.)

"I'm saving my energy for the big haul," I tell him.

"Big haul! You think every day is like yesterday?"

"We're on a roll now," I say.

"I hope you're right!" Foreigner says with a trace of humility.

In spite of Foreigner's eagerness to get on with it, the mood in the galley is relaxed. We are taking a few extra minutes to sip coffee, munch on oven toast, and savor yesterday's success. Foreigner pulls nervously at the hair on his left arm. I ask Paul what was the largest catch he ever made. He tells us that in his forty years of fishing, about nine thousand was tops.

"And those were humpies," he adds, "worth only a fraction of what the sockeye are worth. You have to catch three humpies to match one sockeye."

"Why such a difference in price?" Tom asks.

"Color," Paul answers. "The meat of the sockeye is bright red and it stays red in the can. Humpies—humpbacks, pinks—have pale pink

Tom checks his fingernails while crew look for jumpers. Shame on you Tom! If the skipper notices you – lookout!

flesh that fades when it's canned. For most folks, the red color is more appetizing."

"Color *and* flavor," Foreigner says. "You can't beat the sockeye for flavor."

"In the can, yes," Paul agrees, "but fresh, I'll take the humpy any time."

"For barbecue, give me a white king," Sam says. "You can't beat 'em! With garlic, parsley, oil, salt and pepper—hmmm! You can't beat 'em! Folks who aren't in the know will turn up their noses at white king, but it's better-flavored than red."

"That's right, Sam," Foreigner agrees. "People think the red king tastes better than the white. They couldn't be more wrong!"

"But king salmon is rich and fat. You can't eat very much of it, and not often. Now, you take humpies, they're lean and you can eat as much as you want, as often as you want," Paul explains, defending his stand. "Fresh sockeye is too dry. It's best canned."

"I'll take a nice silver"—coho—"baked in the oven," says Bob, the cook. "It's the best."

"How 'bout the chum?" (dog salmon) Gene asks. "There's nothing wrong with a nice chum. It's my favorite."

"Yeah, chums are best for smoking," Sam tells us. "A hard-smoked chum is better than any of the others, even better than king."

Nels, who had been listening quietly, concludes, "You guys can talk all you want, but give me a nice piece of *lutefisk*."

The galley erupts with laughter.

Foreigner looks at his watch. "Okay, Gene. Start the old egg-beater."

This is my cue to raise the anchor. There's a hint of dawn in the sky as we leave the snug little harbor. As we move through Mosquito Pass, the red and green running lights of other boats follow us like mysterious nomads. We make two sets at

Mitchell Bay, then run along the coastline of San Juan Island toward Henry Island. Foreigner figures the school that was at Eagle Point yesterday will be in the vicinity of Henry Island today. We hope he's right. A few jumpers show along the way, but in places unsuitable for seining because of the unfavorable bottom. At Henry Island we scout the area for a good set. Several other boats are working on the same plan.

The weather is extremely hot, with not a breath of breeze. Henry and Stuart Islands are in what fishermen call the Banana Belt, which has a reputation of being much warmer than other parts of Puget Sound. This long, hot, dry spell has sparked more speculation about El Niño. Some claim that the water temperature in Puget Sound is five to ten degrees warmer than normal, and we hear that more tuna than usual is being caught along the coasts of Oregon, Washington and British Columbia. All this is more like the waters off the coast of California.

The reflection of the sun off the calm water is like a blast from hell. Our eyes smart, our faces are burned, our lips are cracked. Fishing is hard on the hands, even in cool weather; they get chafed, cracked and blistered from working the seine, and the salt water makes every break in the skin smart like fire. We're constantly applying lotions and creams. Paul told me to buy Cornhuskers lotion in Anacortes, and it does help.

There's a showing of fish off Henry Island. We make a set around a couple of frolicking sockeyes. Come time to pick up the seine, and up comes a slender fish about three feet long, gilled in a mesh. Foreigner picks it from the mesh and holds it up, looking puzzled. "Here's one for the books!" he says.

"A barracuda!" Paul says confidently.

"Barracuda? Never heard of a barracuda in Puget Sound!"

"Well, you have now," Paul assures him. "We used to catch 'em on the tuna boats off California. That's a small one. They get to six or seven feet."

After the set we all come down off the seine pile to examine this rarity. It has two rows of razor-

sharp teeth and, Paul assures us, a reputation for using them. "It's a culinary delicacy," he adds. "So we know what we're having for chow tonight," and he places an encouraging hand on Bob's shoulder.

"Baked barracuda it'll be," Bob promises.

Sam is already wielding a sharp blade.

That night, in the lee of a protective point and under more and brighter stars than we'd ever seen before, we savor a once-in-a-lifetime meal. A fish could scarcely be fresher, and the likelihood of having barracuda on a Puget Sound purse seiner is even more rare than finding a barracuda in these waters.

Later we watch a splendid display of northern lights. They're like a hundred searchlights scanning the sky, just over the dark outlines of the island hills. They suggest that something spectacular is going on up north— like the grand opening of a dozen pizza parlors simultaneously.

Bob and I have a quick game of checkers before turning in. I'm now able to provide stronger competition than I was at first, but I still lose. Bob displays a sort of sadistic triumph when he administers the coupe de grace, but I'm studying my "bible," and my turn will come.

I make my way to the bow to check the anchor line one last time before I hit the bunk. As I pass the pilothouse I see Foreigner inside, sitting on his bunk and studying the tide book. A dim light from the far wall silhouettes his hunched form. I hesitate to disturb him, but I give in to curiosity.

"How are the tides for tomorrow?" I ask, stepping into the shadowy cabin.

"Not bad, Raymondo," he answers, raising his head from the dog-eared tide book. "You know, tides are the most important thing in this business. The fish move with the tides. Know the tides and you know the fish."

I'm surprised at his mild manner. Here, one on one, he speaks gently, kindly. He is a man transformed.

"The best fishermen know where the fish will be at certain stages on the tide. By experience

"Seagull eye" Sam displays a product of the 1958 El Nino – a barracuda. A rarity for Puget Sound, it made a good meal.

they learn to anticipate the instinctive reactions of the fish. That's why so much running is necessary. You have to be certain places at certain times."

We chat for a few more minutes, during which I discover a sensitive man who shields his vulnerability and maintains authority by a show of belligerence and aggression. I am glad I let my curiosity overcome my reluctance to disturb him.

Outside, I take a deep breath of the cool night air, wondrously refreshing after the heat and the sluggish winds of recent days. I see the dark silhouettes of a dozen seine boats anchored near us, quiet and peaceful now, resting for another day of heat and aggressive action.

There's something magic about nights like this. I feel as if I have the best job in the world. Can life get any better? I take one more deep breath, then descend into the fo'c'sle.

BLOSSOM TIME

THE FO'C'SLE IS A DISMAL CONTRAST TO the refreshing night air. We've made port only once since the end of the strike, and the scarcely ventilated quarters reek with the combined stenches of fish slime, bilge sludge, diesel fuel, unwashed clothing and unbathed bodies. My shipmates are commenting on the situation.

"Ah," says Bob, inhaling deeply. "Nothing like the sweet fragrance of *Emancipator's* bowels!"

"Maybe they'll digest us all while we're asleep!" says Gene. "And discharge us through the shaft in the morning!"

Tom, as if paying final tribute to the barracuda dinner, contributes an air-vibrating belch, undulating the curtain of his bunk.

Soon, Bob begins to snore. Seconds later, Nels contributes a whistling of air passing through slackened lips.

"Hell can't be any worse than this," I assure myself as I settle down to sleep.

The next couple of days we divide our fishing time between Eagle Point and Stuart Island. The fishing is reasonably good, and we are lucky that we haven't snagged or torn our seine badly enough to cost us fishing time. Such luck is rare, especially when the seine has been fishing so steadily.

Snagging is a common occurrence with some boats, especially those that fish in hazardous places, gambling that the rewards may be worth the risks. It isn't unusual for the crews of those boats to spend two or more days on the dock repairing a badly torn seine, which means losing valuable fishing time. On some occasions, the crews of other boats will pitch in to help, thus shortening the amount of fishing time lost.

A seine "hanging on a snag" is not a pretty sight. Any boat in the vicinity will usually, if possible, go to the aid of the unlucky boat. True, the boats are highly competitive, but there's a strong sense of obligation to help one another when trouble strikes. This obligation is all the stronger if a crew is in danger.

During the course of any given season, misfortune will strike one boat or another, or even several. It is inevitable when four hundred highly competitive boats are battling for the haul. Unpredictable winds and currents, along with the rocky sea floor, increase the risks.

Paul tells of a disaster that he was witness to a few years ago. It was a day such as we've been having of late—calm, warm, pleasant. Suddenly, a freak wind came roaring across Puget Sound like a blast from a giant bellows. One boat, caught off guard, was washed ashore on West Beach. Apparently, her engine had failed while her seine was in the water. Both boat and seine were swept onto the beach. This was the peak of the season, but for them, it was over.

Many disasters have occurred in the waters of Puget Sound. This inland sea, usually tame during the summer months, can become suddenly ferocious at any time. Many seine boats and many members of their crews have been lost in this deceptive labyrinth.

"Shall we run in to Friday Harbor and freshen up a bit?" Foreigner asks the crew after we've delivered our fish the following evening. The answer is a unanimous "Yes!"

We hoist the skiff onto the stern for faster running speed, and make for port. When we reach Friday Harbor, we find others with the same idea. The small harbor is congested with seiners. There's only one shower facility near the dock, and there's a long line waiting to use it. The luxurious hot shower is worth the wait; it's like washing away the accumulation of fatigue and grime and exposing the first-of-the-season enthusiasm. We stay overnight in Friday Harbor, then head for the fishing grounds with renewed vitality.

While we're running, Paul shadow-boxes make-believe opponents on his make-believe ring, the hatch cover. There's a glow of triumph on his weathered face as he downs one imaginary opponent after another, including Willie Pep and Sugar Ray Robinson. Paul's fast-shuffling feet dazzle his phantom adversaries, his style confuses them into a stupor, and he delivers his coup de grace with the speed of a bullet.

He steps out of the "ring" and pursues me. A fast left hook falls short of my nose by a neatly calculated fraction of an inch.

"Ah, my lad," he declares, dancing in position, "if only I was forty years younger, I'd be the CHAMP-EE-ON!"

"No question about that," I agree.

Suddenly he falls prostrate and does forty push-ups in rapid succession, then leaps to his feet and does twenty chin-ups on the starb'rd shroud. We are highly impressed.

By the time Paul finishes his heroics, the *Emancipator* is bucking a strong current through Deadman's Pass. We picked up a Seattle newspaper in Friday Harbor, and now we compete for sections of it so we can get caught up with what's happening in the rest of the world. It's the first time in a very long while that we've had the luxury of being "galley rats." It's almost as comforting as a fireplace on a cold winter night.

A sudden loud pounding on the ceiling ends our short interlude of relaxation. Foreigner has a stick on the bridge that he uses to alert the crew. We call it the devil's rod. Tom and I put on our jackets and, fumbling in the dark, get into the skiff. A fog, rolling in from the straits, is blanketing the area around Iceberg. Minute by minute it becomes thicker, until the lights of other boats are totally obscured. The low shoreline of Lopez Island grows faint, then disappears. Our only clue to our position in relation to the shoreline is the trailing kelp. Its bulbs and long leaves, floating gently on the surface, indicate that the rocky shoreline is not far away. Foreigner stays within sight of the kelp to keep his bearings.

Suddenly comes the blast of the air horn and the order, "Mola lead!" Tom lets fly the buoy and the lead net slowly uncoils and disappears in the gray mist. I am somewhat surprised at this gutsy undertaking, but less so than I would have been earlier in the season. Foreigner's unpredictability has become more predictable.

Tom shouts the order and Nels releases the seine. Corks, leads and web unfold into the misty water. We're laying out much more slowly than usual, as the skipper has to be prepared to stop suddenly if another boat decides to make a set in our fog-dimmed path.

Emancipator's stern soon disappears in the eerie fog, and Tom and I feel like a couple of orphaned pups stranded on a desert of gray. There's a strange feeling of abandonment when the surroundings give you no clues to your whereabouts.

Then, from the gloom, comes a clue. From the direction of the mother boat comes a series of erratic air-horn blasts, followed by loud, quarrelsome voices. They carry clearly over the calm water. Foreigner's voice is easy to distinguish, but why the verbal fireworks? Whatever is going on, it can't be a pretty picture.

Tom and I spot half a dozen jumpers as we wait for the mother boat to complete the circle. She must have run into some difficulty, but all Tom and I can do is wait.

After what seems like a very long time, we hear three blasts from the mother boat's air horn. This is the signal for Tom to release the lead net and start towing the seine toward the mother boat. Every few seconds there's one long and two short blasts, signaling to Tom the location of our goal.

While we're towing, the dorsal fins of two

Late afternoon sun silhouettes crew during pick-up procedure.

killer whales glide into the seine. It is not unusual for the Orca whales to enter a seine, and they almost always find their way out before the seine is pursed. Occasionally, though, a whale gets trapped and, alarmed or panicked, will break through the seine as if it were made of two-ply knitting yarn. The hole it leaves is large enough to frame an average-size house. We are a bit apprehensive until, a few minutes later, the two dorsal fins leave the seine as casually as they'd

entered it—diving and surfacing with slow, easy motions, obviously in no particular hurry. Snorts from their blowholes spew fountains of misty spray and send a haunting sound across the water.

The blasts from the air horn are getting closer. Now the bow of the *Emancipator* appears, faint at first, and soon the two boats close the seine. Tom and I must now search in the fog to retrieve the free-drifting lead. Foreigner gives a blast from the air horn. Its echo gives Tom and

St. Nicholas picking-up on a calm day. Days like this make fishing a delight.

me the general direction of the shore and an idea of where the lead should be. Tom steers an erratic course and we peer intently into the fog. We head in one direction, find nothing, change course, and still find nothing. After a while it seems we must have crisscrossed the entire area, and still no net. Tom's eyes, straining into the fog, show acute anxiety. His entire face reflects his frustration. I am sure he is thinking of the consequences should we fail to find the net. Foreigner would surely bombard us with an avalanche of obscenities, and leave us dangling from the mast.

After running around in circles for awhile, Tom stops the engine and we sit listening intently. Maybe some sound will give us a clue. We hear nothing out of the ordinary. Tom re-starts the engine and we keep on searching.

Finally, after twenty-five minutes or so, we stumble onto the vagrant net. Hurriedly we pull it aboard, and I think we must have set a speed record for picking up a lead net.

Now our problem is to find the *Emancipator*. She could have drifted a mile or more in the strong current, and our range of vision is a scant few feet. We hear blasts from several boats in the vicinity. The trick is to identify ours. We hear a series of quick, impatient blasts. "That has to be Foreigner!" Tom declares. I have a mental picture of Foreigner's fumbling hands pushing frantically on the horn, his face taut with intensity. We head toward the source of the sound, and there, at last, the *Emancipator* appears through the fog.

As we get closer, we can see that the seine is already on board, the bundt is dried up, the brailer is ready and the crew is waiting anxiously for us.

"Where the hell have you jackasses been?" Foreigner barks.

"We couldn't find the lead," Tom says.

"Couldn't find the lead! Couldn't find the lead! Next time I'll tie it to your pud, and then you can find it! Steer your rumps over there and help brail those fish—if they haven't gone belly-up while you two were cruising around!"

It turns out to be a good haul; we brail about a thousand sockeyes.

For the next few days, we divide our fishing time between the Griza and Iceberg. Each day yields diminishing returns. Apparently, the bulk of the run has passed, and all we're catching are stragglers.

Finally, after twenty-eight continuous days of open season, the Department of Fisheries declares the season closed. It's been the longest stretch on record. We on the *Emancipator* are satisfied. We've had a successful season, and in fact, are among the top ten boats of the Puget Sound fleet for gross stock. What's more, we haven't experienced any real disasters. In spite of the long hours, the hard work and the skipper's insults, we've had a great time.

We return to Everett with the proverbial feather in our caps.

THE BIG RUN

EVEN THOUGH THE REGULAR SOCKEYE
season has ended, the purse seine fleet is in port awaiting the fall season on silvers and chums. Some crews, who don't plan on entering the competition, have already taken their seines ashore. Others have taken out a strip or two, as they won't need the full depth of the seine for silvers and chums.

Suddenly, and unexpectedly, the Fish Commission announces a one-day open season on sockeyes at Point Roberts. Rumor has it— there are those rumors again—that the Fraser River system in Canada is already well stocked, and millions of sockeyes are milling around at the mouth of the Fraser in both Canadian and American waters. Seiners can try for the surplus.

Fishermen are usually skeptical about the decisions of the Fish Commission. They think its members are a bunch of desk-bound autocrats who govern their destinies and, fishermen being independent by nature, they don't like it one bit.

"It'll probably be a wild goose chase," Foreigner tells the crew, "but if they're going to open it, we may as well go and take a look."

Tom, my skiff-mate, has already left to go back to college, so the skipper has hired John. John is a veteran fisherman, just back from Alaska's Bristol Bay where he operates a gillnet. He has also fished with many of the Everett seine skippers. He's around forty. He has a powerful physique—close to six feet tall and some two hundred pounds. His big, muscular arms and hands testify to years of pulling a seine over a stern.

Paul will not be making the trip, either. This leaves us one man short, but for only one day of fishing, we'll make do.

"Well, Raymondo," Foreigner tells me, "you're promoted. You're now in the driver's seat of the canoe."

So that's how we'll make do! I might have known! I don't so much mind the idea of handling the skiff alone, but I certainly will miss Tom's moral support when the skipper throws one of his tantrums.

Early next morning finds the *Emancipator* heading north toward Point Roberts, a seven-hour run. The crew is in a jovial mood. We've already had a good season; we're one of the high boats on Puget Sound. We don't have the usual maintenance chores to tend to while we're under weigh, as everything is shipshape. Except for taking turns at the wheel, we're free of responsibilities. We'll count this as a two-day sightseeing cruise, and if we happen to catch a few fish, they'll be icing on our cake.

Bob has laid in some appetizing groceries, so maybe during the next couple of days we can replace some of the upholstery we worked off during our twenty-eight-day August marathon.

Of course Bob, as cook, has his usual chores, but he doesn't seem to be abused. In fact, he seems all charged up, with a spark in his eyes that suggests he's about to pull his biggest prank of the season. We're wise to his repertoire now. He'll have to come up with something original.

I had bought a copy of the *Seattle Post Intelligencer* before we left port, so along in the afternoon I decide to find out how my teams—

This set yields about fifty sockeye in the "bag" or "bundt."

Crew works feverishly to remove fish from bundt and drop them into hold.

Red Sox, Rainiers, Huskies and the Fighting Irish—are doing. Now, in late September, the baseball season is winding down and the football season is just beginning. I spread the sports section out on the galley table and sit, not in my usual corner, but near the door, thoroughly engrossed in news of my favorite teams.

Suddenly there's a deafening explosion beneath me, and my right knee crashes hard against the underside of the galley table. I grab for my leg, thinking it must have been torn off. The leg is still there, but the pain is excruciating. I slump over onto the galley bench, holding my leg and groaning in agony, wondering what on earth has happened. Smoke swirls up from the floor and fills the galley. The engine! Down there below the galley—had it exploded?

Then I hear another explosion. It's Bob, outside the galley door, breaking up in laughter. He sticks his head through the door and asks, "Are you okay? Or should we pipe you over the side?"

"It's not funny!" I moan, clutching my leg. "I think my leg is broken."

It's several minutes before the pain begins to subside. I rise slowly from the bench and limp to the stern to get some fresh air. The entire crew, except for Gene, who's at the helm, is waiting to applaud my recovery. Later Bob, in a more serious mood, admits that a cherry bomb of such magnitude, for that particular job, was a bit of overkill.

We leave Cypress Island astern and travel between Lummi and Orcas Islands. Soon we enter the open water of Georgia Strait. The weather is still favorable. We anchor at South Beach in the lee of the Point Roberts Peninsula. It's open water; usually not good as an anchorage, but the light northwest winds shouldn't be a problem. Now it's only a short run to the fishing grounds.

Bob puts out an evening meal of rib steaks, mashed potatoes and apple pie. It's his peace offering. He has a way of making amends for his crimes, so it's hard to hold a grudge.

John, the newcomer, has now settled in comfortably with the crew. At supper he tells us about his season in Alaska's Bristol Bay.

The Bristol Bay fishery is the best in the world for red salmon (sockeye salmon are known as reds in Alaska). Fleet catches have reached as high as forty million in a season, making this the biggest fishing frenzy on the planet. Some fishermen make their year's wage in the six to eight weeks of the season. They use thirty-foot boats, and only recently have the boats been allowed to use engine power. Before, it was not uncommon to see a cannery tender, which had diesel power, towing ten or more engineless boats out to the grounds. Once there, they were on their own. It was risky business, as the waters of Bristol Bay can get violent in a hurry. The net was picked up by hand, and then came the backbreaking job of clearing fish from the net. It was only the rich reward that kept men going back year after year, and only the hardy ones did go back. John's big, powerful arms and hands testify to the many thousands of reds he has cleared from his nets. Luckily he's a good-natured soul. His hands look as if they could crush a baseball.

"You can have that business," Gene declares. "It's not for me. I'll take a sturdy boat under my feet, and every weekend at home."

It's apparent that Gene isn't likely to make a career out of fishing. That takes a special type of person—one who loves the sea and the boats, and has that certain spirit of adventure, a willingness to gamble.

After the evening meal we gather behind the deckhouse for fresh air and small talk. I'm enjoying it all when Foreigner barks, "Raymondo, did you fix my boots?"

He had instructed me earlier in the day to patch his leaking boots, but in the turmoil of the cherry bomb, I'd forgotten.

"You good for nothing!" he bellows. "Do it! Now!" He throws the boots at me and follows them with a patching kit. The boots are in bad shape, limp and decrepit, with big patches of the lining exposed where the rubber has worn away.

"These boots are hardly worth repairing!" I say.

"Like hell! They're just getting comfortable.

They're good for another season, maybe two."

Gene takes a look at the boots. "Cheapskate!" he says to Foreigner. "We'll have to take up a collection and buy you some new boots. We know you can't afford them."

"Sure," says Sam, "like Mr. Kraft can't afford cheese."

Foreigner responds by lifting one leg, like a dog at a fire hydrant.

I set about mending the worn boots. Sam elects this time to exhibit his claim to fame. He stands on his hands and wobbles around the deck. The contents of his pockets pour out onto the deck—some loose change, a pocketknife, and a couple of marbles. One of the marbles rolls down the sloping deck and through a scupper, gone for good. Bob stops the other marble with a hasty foot. Sam rights himself with a smile of pride, and we applaud his performance.

"Looks like you're down to your last marble," Bob says as he hands it to Sam.

"They are—or they were—my good-luck charms," Sam says regretfully.

"We may as well pull anchor and head for home," Foreigner jokes. "We're hexed now."

"Don't be a wet blanket," someone says. "We're almost sure to catch enough for a meal."

Foreigner takes a long look at the boats at anchor nearby and says, "Don't bet on it. We'll be butting horns with the Point boats tomorrow."

Sure enough, we're surrounded by boats we hadn't seen all season—the *Polarland, Montique, Tajlum, Cape Ulitka* and the rest of the Point fleet.

The Puget Sound seine boats that fish for sockeyes fall roughly into two fleets. About two thirds of them fish the lower sound—the San Juan Islands, Rosario Strait and the Strait of Juan de Fuca. They comprise the Lower Sound fleet. The other third fish the Upper Sound—Point Roberts, Boundry Bay, Cherry Point and Georgia Strait. Of course there'll be a scattering of boats between the two areas. Seiners that fish Point Roberts are called the Point boats. They usually hang a slightly different seine, as much of their fishing is in Boundry Bay and the water there is shallow. Their seines drag along the bottom a lot of the time, and they pick up

a variety of bottom-dwellers such as crabs, starfish, skates, flounders and sea cucumbers. Seines of the Lower Sound fleet, on the other hand, rarely touch bottom, except for the boats that fish West Beach off Whidbey Island.

The Point boats have three areas they fish consistently. They are Boundry Bay, South Beach (the shoreline south of the Point Roberts Peninsula), and West Beach (the shoreline west of the peninsula). The boats run from one area to another according to the stage of tide.

As the sockeye run in the Lower Sound is ending, some of the boats will rush to Point Roberts to get one last chance at the Canada-bound sockeyes. Naturally the Point boats don't appreciate this invasion from the Lower Sound, but it's part of the business. The invading boats are at a disadvantage, of course, because they're fishing in unfamiliar waters.

We wake the next morning feeling relaxed and casual about this whole enterprise. It's been a pleasant trip, a new experience, and that's all we expect. Oh, a few fish, maybe—something to eat on our return trip. The fact that our crew is one man short reflects our holiday attitude.

Poor Tom! Today he'll no doubt be in some stuffy classroom, listening to some soft-spoken professor lecture on some esoteric subject. Paul, who chose to skip this wild goose chase, will probably sleep until midmorning and then read the morning paper as he sips his coffee. How nice!

My elevation to skipper of the skiff gives me the added responsibility of maintaining and running it. During the last couple of weeks of the regular season Tom had drilled me on what must be done, and how, and of course I've picked up some knowledge by careful observation. I should have enough savvy—I hope! I'd better. There'll be no one to help me.

I crawl into the skiff in the darkness of early morning. The sky is overcast, threatening rain. Now, in the latter days of September, we don't get dawn's light until after five o'clock.

As I sit in the skiff, pondering the darkness and a hundred moving lights, I feel disoriented. Foreigner has the *Emancipator* cruising around in the darkness, circling, stopping, and then moving again. Lights from several other boats are doing the same, as if no one wishes to initiate a fiasco. The mood of the fleet seems to be one of indecision. The skiffman, his movements controlled by the whims of the mother boat, can develop a left-out feeling. Separated from the rest of the crew for long periods of time, he becomes almost a forgotten entity.

Suddenly I hear "Mola!" and the crack as the pelican hook releases the skiff. I spin the skiff a hundred and eighty degrees and begin to tow the seine. Within seconds, the dark outline of a boat's hull skims past my bow, nearly colliding with the skiff. I can't recognize her in the darkness. A seine comes flying off her stern. We're being corked, victimized, bamboozled! I throttle an urge to scream obscenities at the ruthless skipper. He wouldn't have heard me anyway above the noise of the engines.

A few short blasts of the air horn, and I stop the towing, release the seine, and return to the mother boat to help hand-haul the seine aboard. What a miserable way to start our Point Roberts vacation.

After sharing our unflattering opinions of the corking skipper, we regroup for another try. We run a short distance and, just as daylight begins to peer over the Cascades, we initiate another set. Nearby, the *Freeland* is also starting to haul. By now most of the boats are in some stage of the set. It's as if that corking skipper had set off a chain reaction.

A northerly wind is blowing, but we have some protection in the lee of Point Roberts. Its bright light, flashing some three-quarters of a mile away, is still clearly visible in the waning darkness. As I tow the end of the seine, a hook shape develops in the cork line—a maneuver Tom had taught me to keep salmon from escaping around the end of the seine. I don't notice any jumpers, so I assume that Foreigner has set on the blind.

After about ten minutes, Foreigner signals me to close the seine. I doubt the wisdom of his decision, as normally a tow lasts longer, but he's the boss. I open the throttle and head for the *Emancipator*. As I am closing the seine, another boat sets her seine a mere few feet from the opening of ours. This is not considered a corking at this stage of our set. In fact,

it's to our advantage, as the other seine acts like a fence, driving the fish into our seine and preventing their escape.

I come alongside and toss the throw line to John on the bow. I notice the crew seems agog, as if they'd just witnessed a walking on the water.

I take my position for towing the mother boat, to keep her from engaging with the seine. I have to shorten the tow line considerably, as the other boat's seine is only a few feet away. Foreigner wastes no time climbing down from the bridge to start his rhythmic plunging. His quickened pace and exuberance with the pole are in contrast to his usual nonchalance. With the tow line shortened and the skiff's engine idling, I listen attentively, trying to catch a word or two about what's happening aboard.

"Inside!" Bob whoops. "Inside" means a jumper is spotted within the confines of the seine. As Sam and Nels purse up, triumphant cries of "Inside!" come billowing from the deck like a rapid bark of a disturbed mongrel. Something unusual must be happening, I think. Maybe Sam lost his last remaining marble. Then again, maybe the crew is pulling some sort of ploy—assuredly on the skiffman, who's the brunt of most jests.

From my position in the skiff the mother boat blocks my view of the seine, so I can't see what's happening inside the floating corks. John walks to the rail, cups his hands around his mouth, and whisper-yells, "They're jumping like rain!"

"Oh, sure," I shrug, my skepticism not allayed by his no doubt feigned excitement. Foreigner hasn't given me any signal, so I continue towing slowly. Usually, when the skiff is towing the mother boat, Foreigner is continually signaling to slow down, speed up, go starb'rd, or go port. His signals are usually vague, erratic and confusing, and would often irritate Tom during the season. He'd be towing in the direction Foreigner indicated, then, seconds later, Foreigner would point wildly in the opposite direction, looking sternly at Tom as if to say, "What the hell's the matter with you! You blind jackass! Pay attention!" Foreigner's repertoire of signals include whirling his arm rapidly in a circle, meaning "Speed up," waving his hands up and down with palms facing down, meaning to slow down, and sliding a hand across his stomach for half-speed. At times the signals came so rapidly, and in such disorder, that Tom simply chose the one that seemed most logical, and it never seemed to make much difference in the results. Tom and I often questioned Foreigner's signals, and suspected he just waved his arms for lack of anything else to do.

The crew begins picking up the seine. Being one man short, with only four to pile, Nels is on the corks, Gene piles the leads, while John and Sam pile the web. I sit in the skiff, towing slowly and picking fish scales off my boots with my fingernails. It can be tedious at times, especially if Foreigner is not performing. Today he seems more concerned with other things. Then, suddenly, he signals for me to release the tow line. Instinctively I run the skiff toward the brailing position. I round the stern and I can't believe my eyes! A good length of the seine is still in the water, forming a large circle. Inside that circle, fish are splashing so wildly that the water is boiling as if in a huge cooking pot. The fish are so thick that many are forced to the surface and escape over the cork line. It's a frenzy of unbelievable magnitude.

Foreigner motions me to the bow to pick up John for help. I respond quickly. John lowers himself from the high bow into the skiff and, showing the coolness of a veteran, instructs me in where to position the skiff. It's a relief to get instructions in calm, understandable English. Quickly we tie the cork line of the seine to the gun'nel of the skiff. The crew on deck dries up the seine to facilitate brailing.

"Don't dry it too much! Give 'em breathing room!" Foreigner yells at the crew.

"That's right," John says. "We don't want 'em to die on us or we'll lose the whole damn lot. They'll sink to the bottom like a ton of bricks!"

The crew starts to brail. Normally the skiffmen help to direct the position of the brailer, but now, because of the mass of fish, the skiff is several yards from the mother boat. The brailer seems woefully inadequate for the job it must do. Its dips don't seem to lessen the quantity of fish in the seine. After eight or ten dips the crew dries up the seine some more. John and I pull web into the skiff to help dry it.

Slowly, as the brailing continues, the skiff inches closer to the mother boat. My hands, which had begun to heal during the few days of rest, are sore again. It's hard work, pulling at a seine laden with tons of fish.

I notice the *Emancipator* is settling steadily. The guard at the stern is already under water.

"Are we gonna be able to take 'em all?" John asks across the water.

"We'll take 'em all if I have to put some in my bunk!" Foreigner answers.

After about fifty dips, the skiff is in position to help with the brailing. I certainly hadn't expected anything like this, so I hadn't put on my oilskins. I'm soaked from head to foot from the splashing of the fish. But who cares! This is a once-in-a-lifetime experience, a dream come true! Hey, Tom, eat your heart out! School is never this exciting! Poor Paul, veteran though he is, he could never have had it like this!

"How many will the hold carry?" Gene asks.

"How the hell do I know?" Foreigner barks. "You think I've done this before?"

Fish are now piled to the hatch coaming and water laps over the stern. I can't help remembering the daylight that showed between the planks while I was working the hold. Those planks are now under water.

"How much room you got left?" John asks from the skiff.

"The hold is full!"

John looks into the seine. "We've still got a couple thousand in here," he says.

"We'll make room!" Foreigner assures him.

"We're sinking now," Sam pleads. "Water over the stern, up to the hatch coamings . . . we can't take any more."

"Put the hatch covers across the companionways," Foreigner orders. "We'll put some in the bow to balance the load."

It seems like madness, trying to put more salmon aboard a boat that's threatening to sink at any moment. Greed could turn this spectacular success into a disaster.

As we keep on brailing, the crew pitches fish into the bow. So much excitement has a way of distorting time. Though the brailing actually took two hours, it seemed like only a few delirious minutes. As John and I run the skiff to the stern, John says to me, "We probably should have released the last few hundred. We're taking a helluva chance!"

The *Emancipator* looks frightfully insecure, as if she's struggling to stay afloat. Her stern is several inches below the surface, and her bow is raised so the red bottom paint is exposed. The northwesterly wind is building waves, moderate so far, that lap against the hull as if trying to pull her under. She certainly looks vulnerable.

The *Freeland*, which set alongside us, evidently had a good haul too, as her crew was brailing for a long time.

John and I tie the skiff to the stern and, instead of climbing up to board, as usual, step down onto the flooded stern. We slosh through ankle-deep water to midship. "I think we were safer in the skiff," I tell John.

"That'll be our lifeboat if this baby goes down," John replies.

"Quick!" Foreigner yells, "Man the deck pump!"

I grab the five-foot-long handle of the deck pump and start pumping feverishly. I'm standing knee-deep in sockeyes overflowing from the hatch. Gene, Sam and Nels pitch fish, also feverishly, from the stern deck to the bow in an effort to raise the stern. Meanwhile Foreigner is on the radio, frantically trying to locate a cannery tender. Apparently the cannery didn't anticipate anything of this magnitude, so there's no tender in the area.

Foreigner comes rushing to the stern. "I called the cannery in Anacortes. Those bird-brains are in there picking their noses while we're out here sinking . . . gave 'em a good chewing. They're sending a tender . . . we'll run toward Anacortes and meet 'em halfway. Pitch fish to the bow! Gene, check the bilge pump! Raymondo, pump 'til you're blue in the face!" (I already was.)

We start running south, down Georgia Strait, at half speed. Foreigner doesn't open the throttle, as the stern tends to lower with increased speed. The wind, from astern, isn't helping our situation. We let the skiff trail about twenty feet behind to reduce its drag on the stern. As I pump with everything that's left in me, Bob pokes his head through the galley window and says, "I hope no seagull lands on the mast! We'd go down like a lead balloon!" Then, looking at the thousands of fish, he says, "I wonder if we can spare one of these for dinner."

"Take your pick," I puff.

"I counted the brailers," Bob says, selecting a sockeye from the multitude. "We had an even hundred."

"And they said the brailer was obsolete!" I mutter without missing a stroke. I feel as if the fate of the boat is in my hands at the moment, so I pump with profound urgency. The water spouting from the deck pump is the color of rosé wine, as the tremendous weight of the fish causes those at the bottom to hemorrhage. We are losing valuable weight, and the longer it takes us to unload, the more we lose. We do, however, have the advantage of the price negotiated to end the strike. The four-cent-a-pound increase will make a great difference with forty tons of fish. That is, if we're able to unload before we sink!

As we move cautiously down the strait we take turns at the pump, each man draining his arm and shoulder muscles in a ten-minute stand. Foreigner seems surprisingly cool considering the stressful circumstances. He sits at the helm on the flying bridge, chewing on a stogy, as if casually on his way to the bank. At intervals he walks to the rear end of the bridge and looks down at the deck load, checking on the condition of his "deposit." How, I wonder, can he act so calm, knowing about the gaps in the seams of the hull planking? Is his composure a mask to disguise his apprehensions?

By now we have pitched all the overflow from the hold and the deck to the bow. The door to the galley had to be shut so fish couldn't slide in. Bob is now a prisoner in the galley. "What a great time," I think, "to reach through the galley window and sprinkle a little pepper onto the stove!" But this is no time for tricks, no matter what the past provocations. We have a serious matter at hand.

After running for about an hour, Foreigner makes radio contact with the tender on its way out from Anacortes. The plan is to rendezvous at Patos Island, a small, uninhabited isle north of

Turntable, the raised platform that holds seine, is only inches above submerged stern heading for Patos Island.

Orcas Island. We get there ahead of the tender and take refuge in the lee of the island. The wind, now stronger, is a real threat to our overloaded craft. We drop anchor and wait.

I ask the skipper if I can take the skiff and run out a short way to get a photograph of the *Emancipator* in this unique situation.

"Go ahead," he encourages me. "This happens only once in a lifetime, and then, only if you're lucky."

I run the skiff out about a hundred feet. From this perspective the predicament of the old seiner looks even more precarious. It's a miracle that she's still afloat. Could there be a hawser from heaven attached to her stern, keeping her from diving to the depths?

I focus my old Conley at the scene, luckily I have two sheets of film left in my pack to record this historic moment.

During times of stress and concentrated effort, one doesn't notice the passage of time or the absence of a normal routine. Now that all we can do is wait, we realize that we're tired and hungry. It's been six hours since we initiated the haul, and still no breakfast. Also, we still have the big job of transferring our precious cargo from the *Emancipator* to the tender.

The cook throws together some pancakes, eggs and bacon. Unable to open the galley door because of the fish blocking it, Bob hands our breakfast out the window. We sit on the gun'nel and wolf down the food, not heeding the countless

Every fisherman's dream: a full hold and deck loaded. The hold is 8 ft. deep, 12 ft. wide and 18 ft. long.

sockeye eyes that seem to be staring at us. I have a feeling that we're alienated from the rest of the fleet, hiding behind this tiny island with our hold full of treasure, as if we're waiting for some mystery boat to come and take our contraband, hand us a wad of greenbacks, and whisk off in the darkness. There's nothing clandestine about what we're doing, but the atmosphere seems to emanate there is.

Foreigner climbs down from the bridge, hollering, "That friggin' tender oughta been here half an hour ago!"

"We've already pumped out a thousand dollars worth of blood," Gene complains.

"That may be what saved us from going down, you knucklehead!" Foreigner barks. "Get below and check the pump!"

Hold full, deck loaded, John, Nels and Gene unload 15,000 sockeye.

As Gene leaves he joshes, "Maybe you and Bob should go stand in the bow to raise the stern."

Foreigner whips off his hat, but Gene scurries out of reach.

All this while we take short, vigorous turns at the deck pump. This constant pumping is necessary, as just a few added gallons of water could very well take us down with our precious cargo. We can be thankful that the weather isn't worse. Georgia Strait has a reputation for choppy seas.

Even under these conditions the crew remains remarkably calm. In fact, Bob seems to relish the circumstances. He sticks his head out the galley window, peers at our load, and bellows, "Oh, you sweet little things! Every one a two-dollar bill!"

Gene, down in the engine room, is keeping constant watch on the bilge pump. Any scrap of kelp or other foreign matter sifting through the strainer could jam the impeller of the pump and cause it to malfunction. That would be a disaster at this point, because the deck pump alone can't handle the volume of water entering the hull.

Finally, the tender rounds the end of the island, heading toward us. We cheer and applaud. All except Foreigner, who, as the tender pulls alongside, erupts with, "About time you jackasses showed up! A slow boat from China could have got here sooner!"

This tender is a stranger to us. She must have been working a different area, so her skipper isn't familiar with Foreigner and his bombastic style.

"Have you been here long?" he asks.

"Long enough to grow barnacles!" Foreigner declares.

"Well, we got here as soon as we could," the skipper says apologetically.

"You're damned lucky this barge isn't on the bottom with thousands of sockeyes floating belly-up in the strait."

The skipper looks remorseful for a few seconds, then surprises us with, "Well, that woulda' saved you the job of unloading."

"Enough small talk," concludes Foreigner, temporarily neutralized. "Let's unload these babies before they're nothing but skin and bones."

We start the long, laborious job of unloading. First we pitch from the hold, which will raise the stern. Stepping into the slimy mess, we sink to our crotches. We work steadily until our heads are below the hatch coaming. After about two hours of steadfast work we pitch the last sockeye from the hold. The seams in the planking, above the water line again after several hours, leak daylight now. No need now to caulk the seams. The chances of their being submerged again are about one in a million.

A few more brailers clear the bow, and we're through. Our score: seventy-five brailers, two hundred fish each, for a total of fifteen thousand sockeyes! At two dollars per fish, our gross is thirty thousand dollars. Each crewman's share: twenty-five hundred dollars.

Foreigner contacts Tony on the *Freeland*, the boat that had set next to us, and learns that she had taken seventeen thousand. Thirty-two thousand sockeyes between us—two of the biggest hauls to come from Puget Sound in modern history, made right next to each other, on the same day. Evidently we'd dropped our seines on one gigantic school that had congregated in the lee of Point Roberts for its final dash to the Fraser River.

One man had left the *Freeland* crew and they'd replaced him with a fifteen-year-old boy from California, who happened to be in the area vacationing with his mother. The lad had never fished and knew nothing about it, but Tony figured that didn't matter. It was just for one day, and they didn't expect to catch much of anything. However, the boy earned twenty-seven hundred dollars in that one day as a fisherman. He'll certainly go back to California with an unrealistic idea of what salmon seining is all about.

We learn by way of the radio that a few boats had made big catches, but none to compare with the *Freeland's* and ours, while many of the boats would have done as well to stay in port.

9

ECSTASY TO AGONY

THE FISH COMMISSION DECIDES TO GIVE us one additional day of fishing. Apparently the escapement has already reached its desired level.

Next morning we head up past Point Roberts to the Canadian line. The skipper figures that the fish blown back past the point yesterday have already been caught, so we'll have to look for a new wave of prosperity. A stiff northwesterly is blowing, and there's a strong possibility that fish schooling around the mouth of the Fraser, only a few miles north of the border, will blow back into American waters.

American fishermen are not allowed to fish in Canadian waters. Markers on shore, east and west, indicate clearly the location of the border. To insure that no trespassers fish north of that line, a Canadian patrol boat runs a continuous vigil along the line. She's a large boat with the look of a military vessel, quite intimidating to the American "enemy." If one of us is caught north of the line with a seine in the water, the fine and the punishment are substantial.

We run up to the line to assess the prospects. There are a few other boats in the area, including the *St. Christopher*, recently returned from Alaska. Slowly we run along the line, searching the water for a showing. The *St. Christopher* is in front of us, doing the same. The rest of the boats are down closer to Point Roberts.

It isn't long before the two boats cruise onto a heart-stopping sight—fish everywhere, jumping like crazy! By far the best showing we've seen all year. The *St. Christopher* spots them first and promptly goes into a set. Foreigner hesitates. All this activity is perilously close to the border, and to make it worse, the tide is flowing toward the border. If we set here, there's a strong possibility that the tide will carry us into forbidden waters. But the wind is coming from the north, opposite the tide, and that's in our favor.

It's irresistible. We have to take the chance.

The *St. Christopher* has completed her layout and is towing her seine—within a few yards of the line and trouble. Foreigner drops the skiff and me a few feet from the other boat. I can almost reach out and touch her guard. As I start my tow I can't believe my eyes: fish flopping across the surface like a pelting hailstorm. I look over into the *St. Christopher's* seine and see the same thing happening. I glance up at Andy, standing on her bridge. He gives me a satisfied grin that reaches, figuratively, from port to starb'rd. He knows we're "in them." I grin back, anticipating another haul like yesterday's. This one, however, is an even better showing.

Where will we put them all? Then I recall our porous hull, and the drudgery of the deck pump. Not again!

The force of the wind can't compete against the tide, which is carrying us relentlessly closer to the line. I study the range markers on the hillside. We're clearly a mere stone's throw from Big Trouble.

Suddenly, out of nowhere, the Canadian patrol boat comes full-bore toward us. The menacing wake from her bow implies clearly that she means business. I look again at the bridge of the *St. Christopher*. Andy's grin of triumph has become a look of extreme concern. Quickly he turns his boat, signaling wildly to his skiffmen to close up. His propeller churns the water as he makes a dash.

Foreigner, from a quarter mile away, signals with the air horn for me to close at full speed. I open the throttle and point the bow toward the mother boat. Looking into the seine, I realize that our concern is two-fold. Not only are we perilously close to the border, but the tide is carrying thousands of sockeyes out of our seine. It's disheartening to have to watch helplessly as all those fish move out to freedom.

The patrol boat slows as she approaches the skiff. Several uniformed men stand on the deck, watching me with scornful eyes. In spite of all I can do, the skiff is inching toward the line. Apprehension grips me. Will they man that menacing deck gun and open fire? At this point they look to me like leftovers from Nazi rule. The patrol boat stands by, only a few feet from the skiff, parallel to the line. If any portion of our gear moves between her bow and the shore marker, we're in for it.

The water inside the seine is quiet, no longer boiling with jumping fish. The massive school has moved to the Canadian side of the line, out of our reach.

We quickly close up. The crew purses feverishly, as I strive with all that's in the skiff to get us out of this pickle. There's excessive strain on the towline as the skiff pulls with all its power against the unrelenting tide. The propeller, turning at the maximum rpms, froths the water as I try desperately to keep the seine and the mother boat from crossing the line.

The patrol boat remains close by, watching . . . waiting . . . .

Then it happens. No question about it. We have been carried into foreign waters. The patrol boat guns her engine and maneuvers alongside the *Emancipator*. A man of rank—he has scrambled eggs on the brim of his cap—stands by the rail and scrutinizes the deck of the *Emancipator*. I expect the worst—their boarding our boat, issuing citations, then securing a hawser and towing us to the nearest port. But to my surprise and vast relief, the officer turns from the rail and the patrol boat backs away and cruises off.

The crew picks up the seine, and all we get from these troubled waters is two hundred fish. Such is the agony and ecstasy of purse seining. One day it's chicken, the next day it's feathers. We head toward Point Roberts, disappointed. I climb from the agitating skiff to the more stable mother boat.

"How come they didn't put us all in jail?" I ask John.

"We made it by a whisker," John explains. "We got purse-up just seconds before we hit the line. Once the seine is pursed it's no longer fishing, so there was nothing they could do."

"How could we lose all those fish?"

"Well, it's easy to be an armchair quarterback," John answers. "If we had that set to do over again, we'd set the opposite way. If we'd done that, we'd be loaded up again."

"But the *St. Christopher* set the same way we did."

"Yeah, and she got just what we did—nothing. You see, the tide carried all those fish out of the seine. If we'd set the other way, the tide woulda carried them into the seine."

When we reach Point Roberts, we scout around for another show. There's no activity. Growing impatient, Foreigner decides on a blind set. We'd have been better off leaving the seine on the stern. We get nothing. It's obvious that the huge school of fish has left American waters and is now out of our reach.

We head south down Georgia Strait running full speed; there's no need to worry today about an overloaded hold. Our destination is home port.

Disappointments notwithstanding, it's been a season to celebrate. Our big haul has moved us up a few notches. We're in the top five of the Puget Sound seiners. Not bad, considering that it's a fleet of four hundred. Our total count for the season is forty thousand sockeyes.

With a long seven hour run ahead of us, the crew gathers in the galley for a leisurely lunch. Nels is topside with steering duty. After lunch is over, Bob announces:

"Well, which one of you boys wants to get beat today?"

He places the tattered checker-board on the galley table with that usual over-confident look on his face. Nobody else seems to want to challenge, so I take the seat opposite Bob. I have been studying my "bible," so I'm hoping it will do some good.

As the game progresses, things are going fairly even. Bob, who normally carries on a conversation with others as he plays, now becomes more aware of the board. Suddenly the crew senses that this game is close, and all eyes become glued to every move.

As the game goes down to the wire it becomes anybody's game. How it happens, luck or Bob's decision to "throw a game," is a mystery. I get him cornered and apply the *coup de grace*.

Bob stands up with a mischievous grin on his face and pats me on the shoulder. "Nice game, Raymondo!"

Of course, I don't really feel like a winner. We still have six hours of running ahead of us, and I'll have to be on careful guard the whole time. I'm sure Bob's scheming mind is at work.

A full moon graces seine boats at 14th street dock in Everett.

EPILOGUE

IT PROVED TO BE A BANNER YEAR, 1958;
the best Fraser River sockeye run since the all-time record 1913 run. Eighteen million sockeye returned to the Fraser in 1958, and twelve million were caught by American and Canadian fishermen. The escapement for spawners was more than adequate; in fact, electric screens had to be installed in some streams to prevent over-crowding.

Because the water temperature was several degrees warmer than normal off the British Columbia and Washington coasts in 1958, the effect of an El Niño, it may have swayed the majority of sockeye to migrate through Johnstone Strait. Normally the sockeye chose to take the longer route along the west coast of Vancouver Island, through the Strait of Juan de Fuca, and then disperse within Puget Sound to congregate again at the mouth of the Fraser.

Whatever impelled the sockeye to take the shorter route on the east side of Vancouver Island is a mystery, but the move was more than welcomed by the Canadian fishermen. During the summer season the Canadians had forged ahead of the American fishermen, but as early fall approached, nature played an important role in equalizing the catch. By mid-September, millions of sockeye had schooled-up and were milling around the mouth of the Fraser, awaiting their final dash to the spawning grounds. Then it came, as if an answer to American fishermen's prayers: a strong wind and tide carried millions of "blowbacks" across the line into American waters. The final two days of the season equalized the catch.

The fishermen's perpetual dream—the bonanza catch, so illusive to so many—finally came true for a few.

THE SALMON STORY

SALMON IS A HOT TOPIC IN THE PACIFIC
Northwest. The declining runs have people pointing fingers. Some say the forest industry is the culprit, logging along streams has destroyed spawning habitat. Others blame the fishing industry, too many nets catching too many fish. Still others are convinced it's TCB's, pollution, industrial and human waste, agricultural runoff and automobile omissions top the list. Then there is urban sprawl taking away habitat and rising sea temperatures. And, of course, there's the dams.

The simple truth is that all of the above are responsible in some part. The sockeye salmon has been an important fixture in the history of Puget Sound. Before the popularity of the orca it was considered the icon of the Northwest. Now the dwindling runs of sockeye have closed the salmon canning industry and limits the commercial season to just a few days a year.

POSTSCRIPT

NICK (FOREIGNER) SKIPPER OF THE *Emancipator* retired in 1983, but still frequented the dock in Everett to scuttlebutt with other fishermen. To the younger fisherman he often recounted the day of the "big load" at Pt. Roberts. I would occasionally take a trip to Everett to visit the dock, and find Foreigner playing pinochle in his net shed with other fishermen. I would sit in for a few games to visit with those I didn't see that often anymore.

His net shed was full of gear from his fishing days that he hadn't sold. Hanging from the rafters was his complete seine which cost about $35,000 to make but today he couldn't give it away. On one wall he nailed a 4x8 sheet of plywood on which he tacked pictures and memorabilia of the past. In his net shed it was like being back forty years.

Nick sold the *Emancipator* in the 1990s. The new owner did a $80,000 restoration on the vintage seiner; it looks great moored at Fisherman's Terminal on Seattle's waterfront where the owner conducts tours on the legendary seiner. In 2017 the boat observed its 100th anniversary.

One of the last of the old time skippers, Nick passed away in 2003. The 1958 crew of the Emancipator have all gone their separate ways. I know of five that have gone to mariner's heaven; two I'm not sure of, and I am fortunate to relate the story.